BIG SUR *to*

California's Dramatic Central Coast

Photographs by Larry Ulrich

Text by Pamela Verduin Cain

CHRONICLE BOOKS

SAN FRANCISCO

BIG BASIN

Printed in Hong Kong.

ISBN 0-8118-1966-3

Library of Congress
Cataloging-in-Publica-
tion Data available.

Book and cover design:
Jim Wageman, Wigwag

Distributed in Canada
by Raincoast Books
8680 Cambie Street
Vancouver, B.C.
V6P 6M9

10 9 8 7 6 5 4 3 2 1

Chronicle Books
85 Second Street
San Francisco, CA 94105

Web Site:
www.chronbooks.com

PEBBLE BEACH, SPANISH
BAY, THE LONE CYPRESS
TREE, PEBBLE BEACH
GOLF LINKS, *the* LINKS
AT SPANISH BAY, *and
distinctive images of its
property, including* THE
LONE CYPRESS TREE
*and golf course and golf
hole designs, are trade-
marks, service marks,
and trade dress of Pebble
Beach Company. All
rights reserved.*

*Images on pages 5,
64–65, 66, 67, 68, 71,
72, and 75 are repro-
duced by permission of
Pebble Beach Company.*

PAGE 1: *Calla lilies, a
wedding favorite, grow
profusely in Garrapata
State Park in Big Sur,
which covers almost three
thousand acres and four
miles of beaches.*

PAGES 2–3: *Natural
designs sculpted in sand-
stone highlight the Sea
Lion Point Trail at Point
Lobos, a starting point for
ten miles of hiking trails.*

PAGE 4: *Bright bougain-
villea edges the corridor
outside Carmel Mission.
Mrs. Leland Stanford
helped raise money for a
major renovation of the
structure in 1884.*

PAGE 5: *The Lone Cypress
defies the changing sea-
sons, remaining steadfast
as if growing out of the
rocks. Said to be the most
photographed tree in the
world, it is held in place
with cement and guy wires.*

PAGE 6: *Brown pelicans
fly in tandem as the spray
settles over them near
Point Piños—point of the
pines—in Pacific Grove.*

PAGE 7: *Gulls and
brown pelicans bask in
the sun on Fisherman's
Wharf, Monterey. Deep-
sea fishing cruises leave
from this pier to take
anglers out on the bay
and beyond.*

PAGES 8–9: *At low tide,
crayon-green algae covers
the walk at Four Mile
Beach at Wilder Ranch
State Park, Santa Cruz.*

PAGES 10–11: *A Monterey
cypress at sunrise, seen
from Lovers Point in
Pacific Grove.*

CONTENTS

INTRODUCTION

Pamela Verduin Cain

There's an old saying on the Monterey Peninsula that residents originally came here either for the golf or because the military sent them. That's definitely true in my case. My father, Richard, didn't play golf; he was stationed at Fort Ord in the early seventies. When he retired from the army, there was no doubt that we would make this our home. I had been in fourteen schools by the time I hit junior high, and it was time to put down some permanent roots. Although we never lived longer than three years in any one place, we behaved like locals during our brief assignments in Missouri, Illinois, Arizona, and different parts of California. During our many moves, my parents made sure my family of five always investigated the local environs, discovering whatever the area had to offer as far as history, natural wonders, and cultural events. Fort Ord was not our wish for our last army assignment, but we didn't realize how kind the Department of Defense was until we moved off post to Pacific Grove. Explorers we became. We read John Steinbeck's works and then walked through the neighborhoods we believed Mack and the boys trudged through. We explored Big Sur by its windy highway, leaning over the cliffs, staring into the ocean below. We went into the Santa Cruz Mountains riding the Roaring Camp Train at Felton, walked through fern grottos in redwood forests, and crunched along the sand of the Santa Cruz beaches. And we trekked through all of the adobes, lighthouses, and other historic spots. The Central Coast is a place teeming with possibilities for exploration. I can honestly say I discover a new facet of this diverse place each year that I live here.

People from other parts of the world seem disappointed if the sun isn't shining during their visit here. But a chilly, raw day when the coastline is shrouded in fog is one of my favorite times to go on an expedition on the Central Coast. The beaches are virtually empty, and you can hear the waves slapping against the sand. A walk through the redwoods in the fog draws your attention to the forest floor. And a quiet sunrise walk when the world is still asleep is a wonderful way to start a day.

Writing this book fulfilled a lifelong yearning of mine to pen a work that would share some of the often overlooked peculiarities of this region. And no matter how many local places I visit or books I read, I always find something new.

Let the lush photographs in this book draw you into this incredible region. If you have a chance, visit these cities and wilderness areas and talk to the locals about what drew them and kept them here. This certainly was the most satisfying part of writing this book for me. The stories I was told brought to life the history of this part of California. I found myself so caught up in the tales of days gone by that I would often forget to take notes. On one trip to Big Sur, my husband, Jim,

SAN JOSE

1 AÑO NUEVO STATE PARK

2 BIG BASIN REDWOODS STATE PARK

3 HENRY COWELL REDWOODS STATE PARK

4 UNIVERSITY OF CALIFORNIA AT SANTA CRUZ

5 WILDER RANCH STATE PARK

6 FOREST OF NISENE MARKS STATE PARK

7 SEACLIFF STATE BEACH

8 MANRESA STATE BEACH

9 SUNSET STATE BEACH

10 MOSS LANDING STATE BEACH

11 FREMONT PEAK STATE PARK

12 THE STEINBECK HOUSE

13 CALIFORNIA STATE UNIVERSITY AT MONTEREY BAY

14 MONTEREY STATE BEACH

15 MONTEREY BAY AQUARIUM AND CANNERY ROW

16 THE BUTTERFLY TREES

17 SEVENTEEN-MILE DRIVE

18 CARMEL POINT

19 CARMEL MISSION

20 POINT LOBOS STATE RESERVE

21 GARRAPATA STATE PARK

22 POINT SUR STATE HISTORIC PARK

23 ANDREW MOLERA STATE PARK

24 PFEIFFER BIG SUR STATE PARK

25 JULIA PFEIFFER BURNS STATE PARK

Santa Cruz Mountains

DAVENPORT
FELTON
SANTA CRUZ
SOQUEL
APTOS
WATSONVILLE

Monterey Bay

CASTROVILLE

SALINAS
SEASIDE
MONTEREY
PACIFIC GROVE
Monterey Peninsula
PEBBLE BEACH
CARMEL
CARMEL HIGHLANDS
CARMEL VALLEY

Salinas Valley

Pacific Ocean

Santa Lucia Mountains

BIG SUR

N

0   5   10   15   20   25

THE CENTRAL COAST OF CALIFORNIA

and I ran across a high school chum who introduced us to some Big Sur characters. These old-timers were almost as much a part of the landscape as Spanish moss draped over oak trees studding the chaparral. They'd seen it all and then some, and they were happy to share anecdotes of life on this raw coast. They remembered a fire that blazed across the landscape twenty years ago as if it happened yesterday. Glowing embers lit up the night sky and tourism took a direct hit during that summer fire in 1977. One off-and-on-resident of Big Sur summed up the laid-back lifestyle of the area with this "unofficial" motto: It is not a sin to put off until tomorrow what would be an unnecessary pain-in-the-neck to do today.

In Santa Cruz, two sisters spun stories of a sleepy seaside village that only came to life when tourists visited. During the Depression "my mother brought in summer visitors to help make ends meet," said Sis Olivieri, a spirited woman in her eighties. "We would make our own wine, crushing grapes with our feet." "We are Italian, after all," laughed sister Rina Carniglia. "We'd go to Hollister and Gilroy where it didn't rain a lot because the grapes were sweeter."

It was also a pleasure to see the private sides of such luminaries as Clint Eastwood, who is as gracious and soft-spoken in person as his Hollywood screen image is tough and unbending. Former White House chief of staff Leon Panetta, who represented the Central Coast for sixteen years in Congress before joining the Clinton administration, displayed a wicked sense of humor and an abiding love for his hometown. And Julie Packard, daughter of high-tech icon David Packard, finds joy in the simple life. When I asked her what she would do if she had two days to go anywhere and do exactly what she wanted, she sighed, thought about it for a minute or two, and then said in a rush, "Probably a combination of going to the beach for low tide on the north coast and spending time in Big Sur."

As different as their stories were, there was one element that brought all these people together. They were all immensely proud of their community. Whether they had been here for five years or fifty, each raved about the beauty and spirit of this incredible place.

Visiting the different cities, drinking in the rich heritage, and gazing at the expansive countryside whetted my own appetite to explore this region even more. I hope this book does the same for your own explorations of the Central Coast.

I was mesmerized by the beautiful photographs in this book, and must thank my friends for helping me to write captions for them during a get together, when we each raved in turn about places we know well. Turn the page to start your own journey.

PHOTOGRAPHERS' FOREWORD
Larry Ulrich and Donna Bacon Ulrich

A spring showstopper: the California poppy in the South Coast Range.

California's coastline is blessed with white sandy beaches, golden headlands, and quiet blue coves swimming with marine life. The beaches are scattered along the thousand-mile coast like a string of pearls in a sea of blue. Just about in the geographic center of it all sits Monterey Bay, the shining jewel of the Golden State's majestic coast.

When we were asked to photograph a book on the region, we were excited by the opportunity to revisit some favorite haunts. We were both raised in the San Francisco Bay Area, and the beaches of Monterey Bay were our playground for summer fun. We were delighted about the prospects of returning to walk the splendid stands of redwoods, watching the migrating gray whales and photographing the ocean landscape.

This photographic opportunity also gave us a chance to do something different. Larry is generally known for his large-format landscapes, but the abundance and diversity of images around Monterey Bay gave him the inspiration to organize his creative energy around a cohesive region, rather than just isolated landscapes. Breaking out of the mold and shooting surfers, pelicans, and golf courses was challenging and fun!

Ever since the days when Monterey served as California's first capital, the region has played an important role in the development of the state, and its rich and colorful past has helped shape the quality of California's present. The abundant resources of Monterey Bay have contributed greatly to California's prosperity.

The environmental abundance of the Monterey Bay region is due to the upwelling of nutrient-rich water in the nearby offshore canyons. A multitude of marine mammals and sea birds are evidence of this bounty. Otters play and feed near the shore, entertaining anyone with the patience to watch. And the pelicans on the pier are always a spectacle of cartoonlike antics and fun.

The wealth of the region doesn't end where the waves meet the beach. The rich, sandy soil of the Monterey Bay area produces fruits and vegetables that have brought fame to the region. In John Steinbeck's day, sardines ran the region's economy. Now an alphabet of crops—artichokes, brussels sprouts, cauliflower—are harvested and shipped all over America. Strawberry fields go on forever, and produce stands peddling local products line the highway.

The Monterey Peninsula has attracted an abundance of artistic talent. Photographers, poets, and painters have always been part of the bay's cultural fabric. Ansel Adams secured a place in history and elevated photography to an art by recording the scenic beauty near his home in Carmel. Tor House, home of Robinson Jeffers, who inspired a generation of dreamers with his poetry, remains an important landmark. Today, in cities like Carmel, Santa Cruz, and Pacific Grove, the arts are supported and thriving, the legacies of their famous citizens kept alive by dynamic, new artists.

The abundance and diversity of the Monterey Bay region provided us with more than enough photo opportunities. One memorable day we photographed the morning light at Big Basin State Park until the fog lifted. Then we packed the cameras into the camper and dashed down to Corralitos to shoot apple orchards by noon. By midafternoon we were in Pacific Grove, photographing the splendid Victorians. After that we hurried to Point Lobos State Reserve to shoot until the gates closed at five o'clock, then made our way down the Big Sur coast for sunset. Whew! What a day!

The last evening we worked on this project we decided to camp at Fremont Peak, a three-thousand-foot pinnacle overlooking Monterey Bay. We thought this usually quiet campground would be a good place to view the evening's activities, a lunar eclipse and the comet Hale-Bopp. It seems that several hundred other people had the same idea. The tiny campground filled, then overflowed. In the parking lot near our camp at least twenty telescopes were set up, all focused on different portions of the sky, and

folks were wandering around checking out all the celestial delights. We felt like we were in the middle of a spontaneous Monterey Bay area block party! We sipped glasses of wine, sampled the evening sky, and chatted with scores of people about astronomy. We finally crawled off to bed in our camper, but the party continued all night. When we awoke the next morning, they were gone and the serenity of Fremont Peak had returned.

At sunrise, we took a short hike to the top of the peak and photographed the first light as it swept across the fog, which lay like a rumpled blanket over the land, obscuring the familiar cities below. When our work was done, we sat down and reflected on the wonderful adventure we had just been on. As the cities emerged slowly from the fog, we realized that we had just spent the night talking and gazing at stars with the citizens of those towns below. Folks from Watsonville, Santa Cruz, and Pacifica had gathered at Fremont Peak for a stellar night, and we were lucky to have participated. We came away from this project with a new vision of a special place with a long history.

OPPOSITE: *The colors of fall enliven a small waterfall in the Big Sur River Gorge in Pfeiffer Big Sur State Park, which offers nearly two hundred campsites.*
PAGES 20–21: *The Big Sur coast expands from Partington Point in Julia Pfeiffer Burns State Park. Offshore lies a large underwater park for experienced scuba divers.*

BIG SUR TO BIG BASIN

BIG SUR

"I've never seen such beauty in my life. Big Sur is like a lover and a friend."

These sentiments are from a current resident. A past fan, an artist, once called it the greatest meeting of land and water in the world. Experiencing Big Sur is like looking at the ceiling of the Sistine Chapel; the experience will be forever etched in your memory and your heart.

Those who have journeyed down California's Highway 1 overlooking the cliffs of Big Sur will never forget the rugged beauty, the isolated beaches, and the sweeping vistas. This natural portrait is only enhanced by the changing weather: Fog, storm, sun, and silent moon each showcases the dazzling coastline in a new light, offering a kaleidoscope of views.

As you head south to Big Sur from Carmel, you first reach Point Lobos, a breathtaking jut of land reaching into the Pacific Ocean and your dazzling introduction to the coastal treasure chest of Big Sur, one that is overflowing with riches. Point Lobos State Reserve is more than a thousand acres of discovery. Silently tread the pine needle–strewn paths under a canopy of trees, under which ferns uncoil serenely. Or hike along the oceanfront trails, either among the sheltered coves where sea life hides or along the craggy cliffs where waves punish the rocks in a never-ending cycle.

Bring binoculars. You'll be amazed at the wildlife you can spot. Sea otters often hide in the maze of kelp at Whaler's Cove. A volunteer docent has set up a powerful telescope here, allowing intimate views of these protected critters. During the winter, gray whales lumber by on their way to breeding grounds in Mexico, sending great spouts in the air as they pass. A hike over the rocky trail along Carmel Bay reveals harbor seal moms keeping their pups close while teaching them to swim. Rabbits hop quickly into thickets of bushes. And then you'll hear them, the barking wolves for which Point Lobos is named. It was originally called Punta de los Lobos Marinos, "point of the sea wolves." More than 250 species of birds and animals live in the park. There are more than 300 species of plants. Spring is a wonderful time to visit Point Lobos—the array of wildflowers is incredible.

The state took over the protection of this jewel in 1933, buying it from the Allan family for $631,000. Originally, Point Lobos was home to Native Americans. Rumsen tribes lived here for 2,500 years. Today, shell mounds and bedrock mortars are all that remain of their vigorous society.

As increasing numbers of settlers arrived in the nineteenth century, the land was taken over and its granite outcroppings became a source of income. In the 1850s, a quarry employing more than thirty-five workers hacked away at the large boulders, sending rock to such places as the U.S. Mint in San Francisco, Mare Island Naval Shipyard, and Monterey's Colton Hall.

In 1862, Portuguese whalers set up a whale oil processing station in the cove near what is now the entrance to the park. This operation thrived until the 1880s when a cheaper alternative, kerosene, began replacing whale oil in lamps. Around this time, Point Lobos also became a shipping point for a nearby coal mine in Mal Paso Canyon. For twenty-five years, horse-drawn wagons carried low-grade ore from the mines to the Point Lobos docks, where it was sent to fuel the nation's burgeoning industries. Not surprisingly, real estate entrepreneurs saw this coastal refuge as a great place for housing subdivisions.

OPPOSITE LEFT:
*A Monterey cypress looms
over Cypress Cove in Point
Lobos. There are more
than three hundred types
of plants found in this
reserve, named Punta de
los Lobos Marinos after
the barking sea wolves.*

OPPOSITE RIGHT:
*Whaler's Cottage houses a
museum, which features
both the history of the
whaling days of Point
Lobos as well as anecdotes
about the state reserve's
appearance in more than
forty Hollywood films.*

RIGHT: *Swimming is
allowed at China Cove,
part of Point Lobos,
also home to 250 bird and
animal species.*

In 1890, developers mapped out areas of twenty-five- to fifty-foot lots, which were to be sold for just $50 each. Thankfully, these were never built.

of the Storm Country; Lionel Barrymore came here for *Treasure Island* in 1934; Alfred Hitchcock directed Laurence Olivier in *Rebecca* in 1940; Sandra Dee and Troy Donahue filmed

A kayaker explores Whaler's Cove, where Portuguese settlers set up whaling operations, in Point Lobos State Reserve. OPPOSITE: *Point Lobos includes 1,200 acres of protected land, 750 of which are underwater.*

At various times, Point Lobos has been home to an abalone drying station, a dairy farm, a cattle ranch, and, in the twentieth century, to Hollywood. Beckoned by the sweeping vistas and rocky coast, more than forty-five movies have been filmed here. The first movie, *Valley of the Moon,* was shot in 1914, and since then some of the biggest names in cinema have come to this forested locale. In 1922, Mary Pickford starred in *Tess*

the 1959 classic *A Summer Place* here; star-crossed lovers Elizabeth Taylor and Richard Burton filmed *The Sandpiper* in 1964; and in 1987, Bruce Willis and Kim Basinger paid a visit while filming *Blind Date.*

That Point Lobos has survived these evolutions ecologically intact is awe-inspiring. Today, the natural beauty is protected so that it will remain unspoiled. Only 150 cars are allowed into Point Lobos at any one time.

*A glowing sunset warms
Point Lobos State Reserve,
which was home to
whaling and quarry
operations before it
became a state park.*

27

Expect delays getting into the park during the summer. Many visitors simply park along Highway 1, walking in to enjoy this protected acreage.

Just south of Point Lobos on the scenic, two-lane Highway 1 is the Carmel Highlands. Famed photographer Ansel Adams made his home here for years before he died. Adams immortalized Yosemite with his carefully printed black-and-whites images, but he also left a lasting legacy of this region of California. He organized the local Ventana chapter of the Sierra Club, inviting roughly two hundred Monterey County members of the Sierra Club's Palo Alto chapter to form the new chapter. The Sierra Club officially approved the Ventana chapter in May of 1963.

Safeguarding the Big Sur coast and the steep forests in the Santa Lucia Mountain Range has long been a goal for conservationists. The Ventana Wilderness covers 167,000 acres and is part of the Los Padres National Forest. It was established through the Wilderness Act of 1964 and is overseen by the U.S. Forest Service. In the Santa Lucia Mountains, steep ridges rise more than 5,700 feet, and v-shaped valleys are carpeted with chaparral. Backcountry hikers will find 237 miles of trails to explore. Through this window (*ventana* in Spanish) one can behold virgin stands of coastal redwoods. On the precipitous slopes at the highest elevations, look for the rare Santa Lucia fir, found only on the rocky outcroppings of this mountain range.

OPPOSITE: *A picturesque view of the Big Sur coast in its prime: lush, green hills, primeval mists, and rolling ocean.*
LEFT: *A grove of coast redwoods in the Santa Lucia Range. The nearby Ventana Wilderness protects 167,000 acres of forest.*
ABOVE: *Deep in the Los Padres National Forest, a coast live oak seems suspended in air. A Boy Scout camp is nearby at Pico Blanco.*

*Hikers who traverse
the Whaler's Knoll Trail
in spring will find
wildflowers such as
these Douglas irises
decorating their path.*
OPPOSITE: *The Big Sur
coast unfolds its beauty
with each curve of the
road, as the seventy-two
miles of California's
Highway 1 hugs its edge.*

The remoteness of Big Sur has discouraged many settlers. The seventy-two miles of Highway 1 that connect the Monterey Peninsula to Southern California weren't completed until 1937. It took sixteen years, $10 million, and convict labor to cut through the densely wooded paradise. Highway 1 soars as much as a thousand feet above sea level in some places and as close as fifty feet to the water's edge in others. In the midsixties, Lady Bird Johnson, the wife of President Lyndon Johnson, dedicated this stretch of road as California's first scenic highway.

Before Highway 1 was constructed, a trip to Monterey from Big Sur for provisions could take up to ten hours. A trip from Salinas to Big Sur would be a two- or three-day trek. The librarian for the county, Anne Haddon, would traverse this untamed land by mule, coming over the Santa Lucia Mountains from Greenfield to bring books to the children on the isolated coast. Some homes in the region didn't have electricity until the 1950s. Even now, it takes a special person to choose to live in Big Sur year-round. The isolated residents are sometimes cut off completely from the outside world during the winter, when giant boulders become dislodged and block Highway 1. Locals wouldn't want it any other way.

"We look forward to [road closures]," says Sola Williams, a long-time resident. "It's so hectic here in summer that it's a time when we have time to ourselves. It gives everybody a time to rest and prepare and get ready again for the summer."

Fire is also a threat in this remote wilderness. The big Marble Cone Fire in 1977 was touched off by lightning during an August storm. Four fires started, two burning together to create an inferno between Black Cone and Marble Peak. Nearly six thousand firefighters worked to quench the flames, which eventually blackened nearly 168,000 acres. It burned for twenty-two days.

"It got so that every day there was nothing but this pall of smoke that extended out over the ocean," remembers Big Sur resident Larry Phelan. "There was no sun, and ashes for days—ashes would be dropping down. At night when you'd be driving home up the ridge, you could see the glow from the fire, even the flames."

The fire danger and the isolation are prices residents willingly pay. Their backyards look onto one of the most spectacular vistas on earth. For most of the year, the fast-paced modern world is only a distant hum. But of course, come summer, recreational vehicles, convertibles, and minivans crawl along the highway, bringing daytrippers and tourists from near and far who want to experience the beauty of the coast's many parks.

Pfeiffer Big Sur State Park, created in 1933, is named after the first permanent white settler in this demanding country. Michael Pfeiffer came here in the 1870s, setting up a ranch in Sycamore Canyon, and his original homestead still survives. There are more than two hundred campsites available to rent, and this park is handicapped accessible. You can also stay at the Big Sur Lodge. Locals frequently journey down the coast to enjoy the swimming at the Big Sur River Gorge, or you can take the Pfeiffer Falls Trail through redwood groves to the sixty-foot falls.

An eighty-foot waterfall is on tap at Julia Pfeiffer Burns State Park. This 3,500-acre park is farther south than Pfeiffer Big Sur. Julia, Michael's daughter, married John Burns in 1915. Together, they ran cattle at their Saddle Rock Ranch, while living at McWay Canyon. In the 1920s, the ranch was purchased by former New York congressman Lathrop Brown, best man at FDR's wedding. Mrs. Brown, who was a good friend of Julia Pfeiffer Burns, donated the 1,700 acres of Saddle Rock Ranch to the state in 1961.

The park's Waterfall Trail is a relatively easy hike through a tunnel under Highway 1 and into a grove full of stately eucalyptus trees on a bluff overlooking the ocean and waterfall. In the unspoiled cove below, the azure water is bluer than Paul Newman's eyes. "It's one of the most beautiful spots in the world," says Larry Phelan, who regularly hikes the Waterfall Trail. "There's no spot on this coast that has both things [redwoods and ocean] going that is that accessible."

Much of this park is underwater. Only experienced divers are allowed to explore the submerged canyons and caves.

From Partington Point, morning glories open to the sun along the Big Sur coast in Julia Pfeiffer Burns State Park.

OPPOSITE: *Monterey cypresses perch precariously on the rocks above McWay Cove, while an eighty-foot waterfall spills* *into the turquoise water at Julia Pfeiffer Burns State Park. The easy Waterfall Trail will take you to this overlook.*

OPPOSITE: *The Point Sur Light Station, now open for tours, was built in 1889.*

ABOVE: *As seen through the barren branches of a Western sycamore tree, Molera Point is a distant destination from the lofty vantage point of the Old Coast Road.*

RIGHT: *The beacon of the Point Sur Lighthouse has been guiding mariners for more than one hundred years, though it became automated in 1972.*

Another popular spot is Andrew Molera State Park, which offers postcard views of Big Sur without the inconvenient hiking of other parks. A wide, mile-long path gently leads visitors to a sandy beach. On the way, you'll pass a meadow lined with sycamore trees that during the spring is also bursting with a rainbow of wildflowers. Primitive campsites are available on a first-come, first-served basis. To survey this park from a different vantage, go horseback riding along the beach or even ride your bike on the three trails that lead to the shore.

Before Highway 1 was built, the sea, lined with dangerous craggy rocks and windswept bluffs, was the most accessible way to reach Big Sur, and vessels regularly moved people and provisions. Notley's Landing thrived from the 1890s to the 1920s. Still, the rough coast of Big Sur claimed many ships, and the area is legendary for its shipwrecks: the Wheaton in 1854, the Ventura in 1873, and the Los Angeles in 1894 are among the most famous, the last taking six men with it.

The promontory at Point Sur is perhaps the most dangerous part of the ninety-mile stretch of jagged coastline, and not until 1889 did it have a beacon to guide sailors. Mariners had to plead for eleven years before they could convince the government to fund construction of a lighthouse. Money was finally allocated in 1885, and the four-year, Herculean task of building the kerosene-lit lighthouse began.

Since there was no highway, supplies were brought in by tender ships. It was an arduous task carting them up the 375-foot rock slope, with the help of a "donkey" engine railway powered by steam. Once completed, the lighthouse's beacon, magnified by a powerful Fresnel lens, could be seen for almost twenty miles. A steam-powered foghorn was also installed to help warn seagoers of the treacherous conditions. Lighthouse keepers maintained the beacon for almost eighty years. But even with the navigational aid of the Point Sur Light Station sitting almost four hundred feet above sea level, there were still ocean mishaps. In 1935, the navy's dirigible the Macon went down, just a few miles offshore. Then, in 1972, the Fresnel lens was replaced by an automated light and the foghorn was superseded by a radio beacon. Lighthouse keepers finally left this isolated outpost in 1974.

For more than a decade, the Point Sur Light Station sat empty and boarded up, a dutiful soldier tending its post but abandoned by its human caretakers. In 1980, it was designated a historic site, and four years later was deeded over to the state parks department.

Now, a dedicated group of volunteers are restoring this lighthouse to its former glory. Guided tours are given of the lighthouse and the keepers' quarters. Sightseers navigate a half-mile walk plus two long flights of stairs to see the restoration efforts. Visitors can also see the tombolo, a geologic formation, on which the lighthouse sits, which looks like a large turtle with its legs and head withdrawn into its shell.

Visitors "seem to have a lot of interest in how the lighthouse keepers and their families lived," says Bob Ellis, a volunteer guide at the lighthouse. "Families had their own vegetable gardens and eventually a cow was brought in for her fresh milk." Ellis recalls that one lighthouse keeper's wife said life at Point Sur was hardest for the children, since they lived on a windy rock with few places to play. A fence was built around the perimeter of the tombolo in the 1890s to prevent children from falling or being blown off.

Today, the most dangerous part of navigating Big Sur is getting stuck behind an overweight motor home or a dawdling driver mesmerized by the view along Highway 1. With its plethora of pullouts and its twisting, turning lanes dotted with historic bridges, Highway 1 is said to the most expensive roadway to maintain mile-for-mile than any other in the world. Most of its bridges were built in the thirties, and they bear names from the times of the Spanish and Mexican land grants. Garrapata (wood tick) and Palo Colorado (red wood) are also creeks that run to the ocean. The most famous bridge of all is the Bixby Creek Bridge, perhaps the most photographed span in the world.

OPPOSITE: *The Rocky Creek Bridge is often mistaken for the Bixby Creek Bridge, which lies farther south on Highway 1. Mile-for-mile, Highway 1 is considered to be the most expensive highway to maintain in the nation.*

LEFT: *Garrapata Creek, named after the prevalent wood tick by the Mexicans who once lived here, makes its way to the Pacific.*

PAGES 38–39: *The Bixby Creek Bridge, along the Big Sur Coast, was the longest concrete span in the United States— 711 feet—when it was built in 1933.*

37

When it was built in 1933, the Bixby Creek Bridge was the longest concrete arch in the world. It's more than seven hundred feet long and towers 285 feet above a small stream. The bridge was named after Charlie Bixby, an early settler of the area and cousin to President James Polk. The artistry of the engineering is evident as one gazes at the symmetry of this span. It took 6,600 cubic yards of concrete and 600,000 pounds of reinforced steel to sculpt.

The panorama along Highway 1 is not the only one, however, and if you want to see the "other side" of Big Sur, take the dirt road at the north end of the Bixby Creek Bridge. This is the Old Coast Road, the route used before Highway 1 was complete. It's ten miles of slow going, but you'll be treated to pastoral panoramas where sheep and cattle still graze. As you climb into the ridges of the Santa Lucia Mountains, vistas of rolling hills frame the churning sea below. This road,

which is unpassable during winter months, takes you back to Highway 1 near Andrew Molera State Park.

Spending the night in Big Sur does not mean "roughing it." In fact, a number of places are eager to pamper you with their world-class service and amenities. The Ventana Country Inn is the area's veteran hotel, serving guests for more than twenty years. This two-hundred-acre complex is thirty miles south of Carmel. You'll find fifty-nine guest rooms snuggled between redwood-laden hillsides and meadows. Most of the rooms have fireplaces and porches with gorgeous views, in addition to a bevy of twentieth-century amenities—coffeemakers, VCRs, minibars, hair dryers, and even warm robes to lounge in. If you feel the need to venture from your hibernating spot, a heated lap pool, saunas, a fitness room, a library, and other spa treatments await. The food is glorious. A continental breakfast and afternoon cheese and wine are included with your hefty room price. You'll also want to experience the restaurant's award-winning menu, featuring an array of elegant meals, accented by fresh herbs and vegetables. Even if you don't spend the night or dine at the restaurant, stop by for a soda just to relish the spectacular atmosphere.

Across Highway 1 just a few miles from Ventana is the Post Ranch Inn, opened in 1992. This very private resort was created to complement the natural splendor of Big Sur, and its overnight hideaways blend right into the rock and earth. The world-class retreat was developed by the Post family, one of several pioneer families who have lived in this area since the 1860s.

Another stop to include on your itinerary in Big Sur is the quirky gift shop/restaurant

Nepenthe (named for an ancient potion used to drown pain and sorrow). The views are the reason to come here, not the food. The site is so stunning that Orson Welles once purchased it for his bride Rita Hayworth, but the pair never lived there.

The Coast Gallery is another must-see. This wooden structure is in the overhang of a cliff and is shaped like an oak wine barrel. Inside, beautiful handcrafted wood items, pottery, and paintings are on sale. There's also a gift shop selling more touristy items such as T-shirts, candles, and earrings.

For a sample of what Big Sur is really all about, visit the Henry Miller Library. An iconoclast and controversial author, Henry Miller is perhaps the most banned writer in the English language; his novel *Tropic of Cancer* was banned worldwide for many years. Miller, who was also a painter, visited Big Sur in the midforties and fell in love; he stayed here off and on until 1962. The library contains books, videotapes, and photographs from the author. Outside, on the library's green lawn, is a display of interesting artwork, including one arresting sight—a huge wooden frame filled with nearly a hundred bicycle parts retrieved from the local dump.

Big Sur today is a haven for artists and people who want to escape the rigors of civilization. "If you are somebody who is artistic or somebody who is alone, you'll never feel lonely," says Sola Williams, who's lived in Big Sur off and on since the sixties. "Big Sur makes you feel like you're with God, and company, and friends. You give up some things to have a lot more riches." And the riches of Big Sur—mountains, forest, meadows, and sea—are masterpieces that will never grow old no matter how many times you visit.

OPPOSITE: *Coast Red-woods, one of two state trees in California, are plentiful in the Santa Lucia Mountains over-looking the Big Sur coast.* RIGHT: *Pfeiffer Point fades into mist during a classic Big Sur sunset.*

CARMEL

Carmel used to be known only
for its picturesque and quaint
village and white sand beach;
today, it's also known as the city
where Clint Eastwood was once
mayor. Visitors from far and
wide often go on "Clint-watch,"
hoping to spy Mr. Eastwood
at one of his two restaurants, the
Hog's Breath Inn or the Mission
Ranch. Don't ask locals to help
you spot "Dirty Harry" or "Rowdy
Yates," though. They jealously
guard the film star's privacy.

PAGES 42–43: *This wide expanse of beach is officially named Carmel River State Beach, though locals call it Monastery Beach because of its location across Highway 1 from a home for cloistered nuns.* ABOVE: *A Tudor-style cottage houses shops on Carmel's Ocean Avenue.* OPPOSITE: *Point Lobos State Reserve, which inspired Robert Louis Stevenson's* Treasure Island, *anchors one side of Carmel Bay.*

Almost forgotten by Clint-spotters today is that Carmel-by-the-Sea remains exceptionally charming, its shops and inns a delightful distraction from a day lounging on the exquisite white sand beach, where waves gently lap against the shore. The city itself, or "the village," as it's called, is just one square mile. But packed into the narrow, tree-lined streets are a plethora of possibilities for the shopper, art lover, or epicurean explorer. Its founders wanted to keep a village atmosphere, so there are no street numbers on houses or shops. Places are referred to by name or as north or south of the main drag, Ocean Avenue. Postal workers don't have to worry about this lack of numeration. There's no house-to-house mail delivery, which has made the post office, first opened in 1904, the place to catch up on the city's happenings.

Eating in Carmel is like eating on a cruise boat. You can't go two or three hours without being tempted by yet another delicacy.

There are more than sixty restaurants to tantalize your palate, many of them truly Carmel traditions. To begin your day, head to Katy's Place—a breakfast stop where locals pay homage to eggs Benedict fixed ten different ways. Or there's the Swiss Bistro on Fifth Avenue, another favorite among locals. "The eggs Benedict and cheese blintzes are to die for," says Beverly Byer, a local television news anchor who comes in so often the waitresses know her standing order. The coffee-klatch atmosphere and the oaklike paneling and dim lighting, more at home in a Tennessee diner than Carmel-by-the-Sea, only enhance the superb food.

The General Store and Forge in the Forest is another popular local spot. Outdoor tables and chairs are tucked in among overflowing planters and bougainvillea-laden fences. And for those who forget that Monterey Peninsula summers can be quite chilly, there's an outdoor circular fireplace where you can warm your tootsies while enjoying a libation or two.

La Boheme, on the corner of Dolores and Seventh, is a cozy bistro with a loyal following. Its European fixed-price menu makes decisions easy, since only one entree is served nightly. Menus are published a month in advance, but there are no reservations, so you

will often find a line snaked around the corner waiting to get in. The Tuck Box Tea Room, down the street, has been a Carmel standard long before the current rage over high tea. A thatched roof and bright canopy lead you to this charming English-style restaurant. Or for your final repast of the day, book a table at one of Carmel's elegant and expensive French restaurants, two of which are praised in all of the dining guides— Anton & Michel and Creme Carmel.

You can feast your eyes as well as your palate in this tiny burg, since there are seventy-five art galleries and studios in Carmel. Sometimes hidden in off-street courtyards, Carmel's galleries display works of all kinds—oils, watercolors, ceramics, furniture, sculpture, and photography. The Gallerie Blue Dog is a popular place for art lovers and those merely curious about George Rodrigue's strange and increasingly famous paintings, in which a surreal blue dog is omnipresent. For those who like humor, stop by the New Master's Gallery to see Will Bullas's whimsical animal portraits painted in bold, primary colors. Ansel Adams lived in the Carmel Highlands for many years, and even though his main gallery is in Pebble Beach, pupil John Sexton's black-and-white images are on display at the Gallery Sur. Some of Adams's works, along with those by premier photographer Edward Weston, are at the Weston Gallery on Sixth between Dolores and Lincoln.

A popular way to explore the galleries at a relaxed pace is to enjoy the "Carmel Art Walk." Every Friday evening during the summer, galleries stay open from 6 to 9 P.M. Artists will often have demonstrations. Blue-and-white banners lead you to the participating galleries. An added bonus is that you might be able to find a parking space because the meter maids—or community services officers, as they're called in Carmel—go home at 6 P.M. Parking is notorious in Carmel. Finding a parking place is as difficult as waiting for a child to be toilet trained—you know it will happen, you're just not sure you're going to live through it. Street parking is free for the first ninety minutes in most places, but it's strictly enforced; once the officer chalks your tires, you can bet an hour and a half and one minute later he or she will be back to write up a ticket.

Art is intrinsic to Carmel, which became a fledgling artist's colony soon after it was founded. The first subdivision map was filed in 1902 by Frank Devendorf; the city's founder is immortalized with a city park named in his honor on the corner of Ocean Avenue and Junipero. Just three years later, in 1905, a group of residents formed the Arts and Crafts Club, which might have remained a typical community cultural center except for the intervention of Mother Nature. The Great Quake of 1906 devastated San Francisco, whose community of artists, writers, and musicians suddenly had no place to live. Many decided the tranquillity of the cypress trees and white sand beaches of Carmel would be the perfect inspiration for their creativity, and this migration molded Carmel's image as a bohemian arts colony.

The group of writers and poets who came to Carmel included novelists Mary Austin, Jack London, Upton Sinclair, and Sinclair Lewis, as well as poet George Sterling. The poet/playwright Robinson Jeffers also chose Carmel for his home, moving to the area in 1914 and staying until his death in 1962. He bought a five-acre site near Carmel Point and began building Tor House. He studied the stone-masons who worked on his home and was

A flash of fall color shimmers in the village of Carmel, which for many years was considered a bohemian arts colony.

soon pitching in himself. He single-handedly built the Hawk Tower (named after a bird that circled overhead) for his wife, Una. It was there that he would lock himself away to write. Jeffers's lyrical descriptions of Big Sur capture the many moods of this temperamental coastline. The Tor House is now open for tours. It's registered with the National Trust for Historic Preservation.

Music and theater are also important parts of Carmel's art world. In 1910, the Forest Theater was founded, becoming California's first outdoor theater. They produced Shakespearean dramas and pageants by local play-

wrights, with almost all of the townsfolk taking part. The Western Drama Association and Forest Theater Society were lauded by critics in San Francisco and Los Angeles, and today you can still enjoy stage productions under the stars and the towering trees during the summer months. Recently, the theater group expanded its repertoire by showing classic films, many of them shot on the Monterey Peninsula. Movies such as *National Velvet, Turner & Hootch,* and *Play Misty for Me* elicit cheers from locals, who come as much to see their local scenery dressed up by Hollywood as for any of the famous actors and actresses. Fans of the Forest Theater often bring a picnic dinner to munch on dur-

ing the movie, wrapping themselves in blankets and layers of clothes to protect against the fog-filled nights. Roaring fires in pits near the auditorium don't create a lot of warmth, but they add to the ambiance, and more than one slumbering patron has been sharply awakened by the tiny embers that occasionally pop out of the fire.

Those same early residents who originally formed the Arts and Craft Club also built a theater in 1922, where the current Golden Bough Playhouse now stands. The first theater, located on Ocean Avenue, burned down in 1935 after a production of *By Candlelight.* The playhouse was moved to a new site and lovingly restored. Then, with an irony that would only be plausible in real life, the second facility burned again after a production of—you guessed it— *By Candlelight.* Rebuilt in 1950, this building has come full circle. Once a movie theater, it was recently purchased by the Pacific Repertory Theater, which now uses it again for stage performances. No word yet if *By Candlelight* will ever be on the schedule.

Finally, perhaps the preeminent event in Carmel is the three-week Bach Festival, which runs from the last two weeks of July through the first week of August. The best musicians from all over the world come to play baroque masterpieces under the direction of Maestro Bruno Weil. The festival was started in 1936 by Miss Dean Denny and Miss Hazel Walraus, who owned the Denny-Walraus art gallery.

When you've had enough sunning, eating, and art gazing, it must be time to shop, and in Carmel you can find everything from aviation to toy stores, with enough variety to

LEFT: *A white picket fence surrounds a white-washed cottage in Carmel. The village has just four thousand residents, but more than one million tourists visit each year.* OPPOSITE: *Stores hang their shingles, beckoning shoppers on Ocean Avenue, Carmel's main drag.*

A mound of kelp on Carmel River State Beach, a popular place for bonfires and picnics. OPPOSITE: *This house under the trees on Scenic Road in Carmel-by-the-Sea would be at home in the British Isles.*

leave your imagination spinning. It's a town especially suited for those who have everything, since its many specialty shops are sure to offer you plenty of things you've never seen before. But there's an important Carmel law on the books that should be remembered when hitting the pavement in search of that perfect gift. A city ordinance adopted in 1963 prohibits people from wearing high-heeled shoes on the street or sidewalks. Of course, you can buy high-heeled shoes in one of the half dozen or so shoe stores in town, and then you can stop at city hall and get a permit to wear them. "It's a health and safety issue and that's the truth," says Sarah Manning, a Carmel city employee.

What you won't find in Carmel is a Wal-Mart or Walgreen's. The only chain stores that

have managed to find a home in Carmel-by-the-Sea are upscale shops such as Sharper Image and Banana Republic. In fact, Carmel's current battle to keep the chains at bay is only the latest struggle to maintain the quaint village atmosphere that drew people in the first place. Long-timers want to preserve that famous village atmosphere and don't want the tarnish of tackiness to pervade the cozy cuteness of Carmel.

No issue is too small to escape notice. Storekeepers are admonished that no more than 10 percent of their merchandise can be decorated with the word "Carmel" or other place names. A few T-shirt stores have been granted a special dispensation from city hall to go over the limit, but T-shirt vendors are afraid their wares may go the way of the ice-cream cone in Carmel. A few years ago, the city council banned people from eating cones on the streets as part of a larger effort to curtail fast-food outlets.

"We want unique stores," says Mel Kline, who headed up a task force on chain stores in the village. "We don't want the mom-and-pop stores squeezed out by chain stores who can afford to take a loss and just come here for image." This twenty-eight year resident wants "to bring it back to the charming village it used to be."

With more than one million people sojourning to Carmel each year, maintaining a village atmosphere is a difficult task. Almost 30 percent of the budget comes from hotel taxes, while almost another third comes from sales taxes, so resident are aware of how important tourists are to the local economy. The city wouldn't survive without those out-of-towners and their credit cards. It means locals can't be ambivalent about the forces shaping their community. So long-time residents focus their energy on keeping the generic national chains from streamrolling home-grown entreprenuership and turning their town into one more mall.

It's a fight as old as Carmel. Those same artists who flocked to the idyllic enclave in the early part of this century were not thrilled when others began invading "their" paradise. Concerned about development and the threat to their lifestyle, residents voted to incorporate in 1916 to protect the area. In fact, one artist group even sued the city trustees to prevent Ocean Avenue from being paved.

But commercial interests persevered and soon developers proposed a huge Spanish-style hotel right on the waterfront. Citizens responded with outrage and launched an all-out campaign to stop the development. Banding together, residents bought a large section of the beachfront property, vowing to preserve it always. In fact, in 1929 a zoning ordinance was adopted that states business development will be subordinate to the residential atmosphere. Electric signs were prohibited and street lights and sidewalks were discouraged. One candidate running for election that year proclaimed that he'd work hard to keep Carmel *off* the map.

Carmel is very much on the map today, but residents still pressure city hall to keep gaudiness at bay. Even if they can't keep out the chains entirely, rest assured that protectionists will prevent chain stores from looking like chain stores. No giant golden arches or neon signs advertising two tacos for ninety-nine cents will be seen in Carmel-by-the-Sea.

And, indeed, the most charming places to stay in town are locally owned. One of the most famous is the Cypress Inn, owned by Carmel Valley resident and star of the silver screen Doris Day. The hotelier and star of all of those *Pillow Talk* movies encourages her guests to bring their pets. A visit to the bar in the late afternoon will find overnight guests sipping glasses of white wine, their dogs lying contentedly at their feet. Invariably, the dogs become the center of attention. "He's such a water dog," says one woman, gently stroking her retriever's head. "When I get into the shower, he just looks at me so plaintively." Each dog—there's a limit of two per guest—costs an extra $17 a night.

The village of Carmel has more than fifty inns, ranging from delightful bed-and-breakfasts to the imposing Highlands Inn, where the most famous chefs in the world come for the "Masters of Food and Wine" symposium.

The lights of Pebble Beach shine under violet skies over Carmel Bay.

Though tourism is the lifeblood that sustains Carmel, the town is also a place of historical significance. On the grounds of the Carmel Mission, the true birthplace of Carmel, you'll find the remains of Father Junipero Serra. The diminutive padre, who was only five feet two inches tall, helped lead the famed Portola expedition to rediscover the lovely Monterey Bay, which the explorer Viscaino had raved about 167 years before. Father Serra founded the mission in Monterey in 1770 but moved it to Carmel the following year. The San Carlos de Borromeo de Carmel Mission was the second mission established in California, and it was one of the most special in a chain of twenty-one missions that spanned the Golden State, all one day's walk apart.

Father Junipero Serra, who was already fifty-seven when he came to the peninsula, wanted to spread Catholicism throughout California. He stayed in the Carmel Mission and started his conversion efforts among the Native American Rumsen tribes, who had lived here for five thousand years. In addition to feeding souls, the friar wanted to feed their bodies. His goal was to make the mission self-sufficient, so Serra, with his friend and master gardener Father Palou, planted a large vegetable garden with lettuce and artichokes, which today are major crops in the Salinas Valley. Mission records show that in 1774 the padres harvested from the nearby Carmel Valley 207 bushels of wheat, 250 bushels of maize, and 45 bushels of beans. Livestock also roamed the surrounding fertile lands.

Father Serra died at the mission in 1784, just four days before his seventy-ninth birthday. It was his thirty-sixth year of missionary work, and, according to his wishes, he was buried at the mission that had been his headquarters. The missions were secularized in 1833.

In 1879, Robert Louis Stevenson wrote about his visit to Carmel Mission, which was then in ruins. Just three years later, the priest at Monterey's Royal Presidio Chapel discovered Serra's grave and an all-out restoration project began. Mrs. Leland Stanford headed the restoration committee, and the new Carmel Mission was rededicated in 1884, one hundred years after Father Serra's death. Another massive restoration took place in the 1930s, led by Hugh Downie, who restored it to its original appearance. Today, the mission is ranked a basilica, meaning that it has ceremonial privileges but is not a Catholic church. It is also a National Historic Landmark.

CARMEL VALLEY

If you wander up the Carmel River, which flows just a short distance from the mission, you'll head into the long, narrow Carmel Valley, which occupies about sixty-four thousand acres of bucolic land. This unincorporated part of Monterey County had its roots in the huge land grants given in the 1830s by Governor Alvarado. Massive acreage, sometimes as much as eight thousand acres, were given to families who had served the government well.

The Boronda family was one of the first to actually inhabit their rancho in the 1840s. Legend has it that after her husband was injured in a ranch accident, Doña Maria Boronda began making *queso del país*— cheese of the nation—to support her many children. Peninsula land baron David Jacks is said to have discovered this tasty white cheese and encouraged other dairy farmers to produce it as well. Soon, this cheese became known as Monterey Jack cheese. The adobe where the family lived can still be seen today, beautifully restored as a private residence.

Carmel Valley, ringed by the Santa Lucia Mountains and the Peninsula Ridge, is a more pastoral area where cattle ranches and dairy farms were once key livelihoods for residents. The weather in this region is much warmer than on the peninsula, and it also has a great microclimate for orchards. For example, in the 1870s, Edward Berwick got some cuttings from the orchards at the mission, and soon his green thumb became famous the world over as his Winter Nelis pears were shipped by the carload to London and Europe. He also was praised for his apple and walnut groves.

PAGES 56–57: *Artichokes grow along Highway 1 near the Carmel River. This large, rotund vegetable is a multi-million dollar crop in Monterey County.*
LEFT: *Coast live oak trees dot the rolling hills of Carmel Valley.*
OPPOSITE: *Carmel Valley rolls into the hills of Tularcitos Ridge. This land was first settled by families given huge land grants from Mexico in the 1800s.*

Another gentleman farmer and perhaps the most famous native son of Carmel Valley is former White House chief of staff Leon Panetta. He was ecstatic to return home to the Monterey Peninsula in January 1997, after helping to elect President Bill Clinton to a second term. "I've got twelve acres of walnuts, and the orchards are saying, it's about time," says Panetta, who glows when he talks about his hometown. "It's good to be home. I got the chance as chief of staff to crisscross the nation, particularly in the last campaign. And the most beautiful place of all is the Central Coast. It's the diversity of the people and the diversity of the beauty, from the agricultural fields to the coast."

Today, Carmel Valley is more known for its golf courses and exclusive homes than its cattle and fruit trees. There are several popular courses, some public, some private, as you drive out Carmel Valley Road. There are also many exclusive resorts and inns that have hosted weekend getaways for the rich-and-famous, such as Andre Agassi and Brooke Shields, who rented out several exclusive inns for their April 1997 wedding.

As in Carmel-by-the-Sea, many valley residents now are trying to protect the family atmosphere found in the rolling hills. A development proposal for twenty thousand acres was shot down in a recent election. Partners for the Rancho San Carlos project had proposed a "preserve" of eighteen thousand acres, but opponents said the homes, golf courses, restaurants, and stores were scattered all through the development, negating the protection of the habitat. This is the same land that was once owned by East Coast millionaire George Moore, who bought the twenty-two thousand acres in

OPPOSITE: *The Carmel River flows past the private Carmel Valley Ranch Golf Course, one of several golf courses in the valley.*

1923 and planned a thirty-five room mansion for his family. An avid sportsman, Moore introduced Russian boars for his guests' hunting enjoyment, and today, wild pigs can still be spotted. But the stock market crash of 1929 bankrupted Moore and his dreams went unrealized.

The county-run Garland Ranch Park covers forty-five hundred acres and offers panoramic views for hikers and nature lovers. Visitors will also find Native American artifacts on display. Not surprisingly, much of this terrain was donated to the county as a way to buffer the valley against development.

Concern for the environment is shared by all residents along the Central Coast. For example, there are more than thirty-two thousand trees in Carmel village, and no city-owned tree can be cut without a review by the city's

Forestry Committee. Committee members actually look at any offending limbs or trees personally on a monthly tree tour. The latest hazard to the forests in and around Carmel is a disease called pine pitch canker. It's attacking the native Monterey Pines and whole stands are dying. Already six hundred pine trees within the square-mile city limits have been affected. Living up to its name as a tree city, Carmel has budgeted money for an experiment to save the trees. "We are raising seedlings, approximately a thousand trees," says Parks, Beach, and Forest Supervisor Mike Branson. "We're trying to treat the trees with the canker to see if they're resistant. We're looking toward the future and trying to replace those trees that die."

This ecologically sensitive perspective makes Carmel-by-the-Sea a mecca for those who want to enjoy lush beauty and luxurious surroundings in an artistically vibrant community.

The Hottentot fig, a South African native plant, covers the sandy shore where a creek meets the sea at Carmel Bay.

PEBBLE BEACH

From its earliest years, Pebble Beach has been a playground for those who want to get away from it all. Its white sand and curving pebbled beaches are its sandboxes. The groves of trees are nature's jungle gym, the magnificent wooded areas intersected by black-top roads. Viewing the grandiose mansions built behind massive fences is like riding the merry-go-round; as your car curves around, you crane your neck, looking for the best view of hidden homes.

As you approach the guardhouse at any of the five entrances to Pebble Beach, reset your odometer as you begin your journey on the famous 17-Mile Drive. You'll have to make a complete loop of the well-marked road to tally the complete seventeen miles, including a few switchbacks to sneak in another view or two. Originally, this famous drive started at the Hotel Del Monte in Monterey. Railroad pioneer Charles Crocker constructed the hotel in the 1880s as a world-class seaside resort, then he built a road to take his wealthy guests from the luxury of the hotel to the then-primitive wonder of the woods and sea, now the Pebble Beach Resorts. The roundtrip then was closer to thirty-five miles. Historic photographs show that women and men trekked in their Victorian garb to the pine forests or to the sandy shore to picnic or stroll along the water's edge. Even then, visitors who arrived in horse-drawn carriages were asked to "pony up" a fee to enjoy the splendor of nature. In 1914, the toll was twenty-five cents for a vehicle that carried fewer than three people. Today, cars and trucks pay seven dollars more to zigzag through this unincorporated portion of Monterey County.

The ocean views aren't as spectacular as Big Sur's, but visitors also come to see the mansions and estates. "The first time my husband took me on the drive, he asked if I wanted to see the big houses," remembers Lorraine Brown-lee, who came to live in Pebble Beach in 1970. "The first time I just saw a lot of big fences." Weekends and holidays will find

PAGES 64–65: *From Cypress Point along 17-Mile Drive you can see Point Lobos in the distance, all part of the Monterey Bay National Marine Sanctuary, which covers one quarter of the California coast.*
LEFT: *At day's end, the sun melts into the foamy Pacific, here viewed from Pescadero Point on 17-Mile Drive in Pebble Beach.*
OPPOSITE: *Waves leap over the rocks at Sunset Point, glimpsed from Cypress Point Lookout along 17-Mile Drive.*

dozens of cars waiting to pay the toll to view the sights behind the gates. It's easy to follow along the drive, as it is marked with red-and-gold stripes, leading you past some glorious spectacles.

If you enter through the Pacific Grove gate, you'll see the newest of the hotel/resort complexes, the Inn and Links at Spanish Bay, built by the Pebble Beach Company, which owns the fifty-three acres of Pebble Beach. The golf course is in the style of a links-land course from Scotland, and to perpetuate the Scottish mood, a lone bagpiper dressed in a kilt strolls through the grounds each evening, serenading hotel guests and golfers. The course was designed by Robert Trent Jones, Jr., Tom Watson, and Frank "Sandy" Tatum. In addition, you'll find championship tennis courts, exercise facilities, a pool, and the requisite "shoppes," including the Ansel Adams Gallery.

Those who can't afford to stay at the Inn at Spanish Bay (and with room rates ranging from $305 to $2,000 a night, that would be most of us) will relish the open spaces and pull-outs on the drive, which allow unfettered views of the Pacific. Interpretive signs relay the history of the area, which reaches back to the days when Juan Portola camped in 1769 while trying, in vain, to rediscover the lauded Monterey Bay.

You'll want to stop at the Restless Sea, one of the many pullouts on the Drive. Here, the sea is indeed restless, churning turbulently and sending waves of salt spray in the air even on calm days. There are conflicting explanations for this upheaval. The full-color brochure says that several ocean currents collide here, but the posted sign says it's more likely that submerged reefs churn up the sea.

The rocky Point Joe is another great stopping point. This outcropping of boulders halfway submerged in the roiling ocean has often been mistaken for the entrance of the sheltered Monterey Bay. Human lookouts on top of massive schooners, steamships, and sailboats have sometimes realized too late their mistake, and many a ship has been ripped by these rocky shores. Many tourists have been disappointed, too, after paying their toll to see the magnificent views. This part of the peninsula is often shrouded in fog, which has its own beauty, though not necessarily the one that you would pay to see.

To enjoy the birds and animals that congregate on the shore, stop at the Bird Rock vista point. Just offshore, sea lions and harbor seals cavort on large hills of granite. Telescopes set up in the parking lot allow you to get a close-up look at the animals as they lumber out of the water and dry themselves in the sun. You'll no doubt hear their barks as they protect their piece of the rock. Across from this area is the Bird Rock Hunt Course, which, prior to World War II, was a training ground for the 11th Calvary, who practiced riding and combat with their sabers.

Pebble Beach is as much a showplace of man-made structures as it is of natural creations. The homes on 17-Mile Drive are spectacular architectural monuments, some sitting back among pine trees and oaks, blending in with their natural environment. Other estates, more recently built, are imposing, with four-car garages, walls of windows, and enough square footage to house the entire San Francisco Giants baseball team. Whimsy graces several estates: the cottagelike house near Fanshell Beach looks as if Hansel and Gretel might play under the patchwork quilt roof, nestled into the sand dunes.

A view of famous white-capped Bird Rock on 17-Mile Drive in Pebble Beach. Many folks set up telescopes here to view the birds and sea life on the rocks.

There's the house locals dubbed Clamshell House, where five Quonset-hut-shaped ovals curve so that virtually every room has a view of dramatic Cypress Point. Snuggled next to the private Cypress Point Golf Course is a house where there's never a wait to get on the green. The homeowner has designed a putting green complete with flag right in the front yard.

Golf, of course, is king in Pebble Beach. There are the private courses: Monterey Peninsula Country Club's Dunes and Shore Courses and the elite greens of Cypress Point. And then there are the ones owned by the Pebble Beach Company, open to the public but reserved for the upper-echelon golfer who can afford to swing on these hallowed fairways. Pebble Beach Golf Links is the most famous, but Spyglass Hill and Spanish Bay are on a par when it comes to difficulty and beauty. Guests staying at the resorts can pay as little as $150 to play Spanish Bay, while nonresort players have to fork over $275 plus the $25 cart fee to tee off on the eighteen holes of Pebble Beach.

The emerald-green courses are in the spotlight during the first weekend in February when the AT&T Pebble Beach National Pro-Am is played. This extravaganza is not just for golfers. It's for star-gazers, too, who come from across the country to see the stars of film, song, and television paired with the sportsmen of the greens. It was the old crooner himself, Bing Crosby, who started this tournament. An avid golfer, Crosby started the tourney in Rancho Santa Fe in the San Diego area in 1937. He moved it to the Monterey Peninsula in 1947, doubling the winner's purse to $10,000. That became the

start of a long tradition of golf and stars in The Crosby, also called the Clambake.

Some of the world's greatest names in golf have triumphed over the elements to win this tournament. Ken Venturi and Billy Casper were winners in the early sixties, and in the seventies you would have seen the names Jack Nicklaus, Johnny Miller, Ben Crenshaw, and Tom Watson on top of the leader board. But in the last decade or so, at the AT&T, golf fans have marveled at Mark O'Meara, who has captured the top spot more than anyone else, in 1985, in '89, '90, and in '92. In 1997, record attendance was tabulated when Tiger Woods, matched up with actor Kevin Costner, hit the links. Golfing sensation Woods roared back from a shaky start and almost caught the winner, Mark O'Meara, who won the tourney for a record fifth time.

The weather has always been a major factor, affecting who wins and who loses at this winter tournament. Rain has shortened the tournament numerous times. And snow has even fallen, turning the greens white in 1962. During the drought years of the late seventies, locals looked forward to the Crosby, since that meant rain was sure to come. But for Bing's last Clambake in 1977, the weather was beautiful every day, and even the wind was silent. Bing died the same year, and in 1978 his son, sixteen-year-old Nathaniel, stepped in to act as tournament host. The first round was washed out completely that year in true "Crosby" fashion. In 1986, with new title sponsor AT&T, the second round was canceled altogether. And a make-up Monday was also rained out, so the tournament was shortened to just fifty-four holes.

Some spectators may come for the golf, but most come to see the amateurs, who may carry handicaps in the world of golf but are at the pinnacle of success in other fields. The early years saw such Hollywood legends as Dean Martin, Bob Hope, and Phil Harris charm the crowds. Later, youngsters lined up along the fairways with autograph books trying to garner the signatures of Tennessee Ernie Ford, Willie Mays, John Brodie, and Doug McClure. Actor Jack Lemmon has never made the cut in the more than twenty tournaments he's participated in. His partner at the AT&T, pro Peter Jacobsen, has said he'd rather have Jack make the cut than win the tournament himself. Sightseers got more than the price of admission in 1992 when comedian Bill Murray joined the amateur ranks of the contest. The often-irreverent star of *Groundhog Day* and *Caddyshack* has brought new fans to Pebble Beach with his outlandish behavior and clothing.

In the early sixties, a young actor appeared on a local television show and was teased on-air about not being invited to play at the Crosby. "We were talking about golf," recalls Clint Eastwood today, whose TV alter ego at the time was Rowdy Yates on the western television series *Rawhide.* "It might have been John Cohan [the owner of the station] who asked me, 'How come you're not playing in the tournament?' I said, 'I don't know; I guess they don't like cowboys.' Everyone laughed, and I didn't think too much of it. But the next year I got an invite to the tournament, with a P.S. saying 'We do like cowboys.' It was signed Larry Crosby [Bing's brother and tournament director]. He just happened to be watching the show that night and got a laugh out of it."

Eastwood, who is now a Hollywood legend both in front of and behind the camera, played in his first Crosby in 1965. He now travels a short distance from his home in the area to take part in the annual tournament. He first came to the Monterey Peninsula during an army stint in the fifties. "I thought if I ever had a few crumbs, I'd like to live and settle here." The Academy Award-winning director, who has starred in more than forty films, did collect a few "crumbs" in those intervening years and has lived here for decades, winning the mayorship of Carmel in 1986. He's been a perennial favorite at the AT&T ever since.

Pebble Beach and its beautiful environs also host a number of key events that have nothing to do with golf. The Equestrian Center has seen many four-legged champions pound its turf. And every year some of the most handsome dogs in the nation gather at The Lodge to participate in the Del Monte Kennel Club Dog Show. The Lodge also rolls out the red carpet in August for vintage automobiles, part of the Pebble Beach Concours d'Elegance car show. Jaguars, Rolls-Royces, Hispano-Suizas, and Bentleys from eras gone by dazzle spectators with their gleaming chrome as they sit in dignified long rows while waves gently brush against the rocks below.

The many moods of the sea are framed by windswept cypress trees along the coastline. Perhaps the most photographed tree of all time is along the 17-Mile Drive. The Lone Cypress is said to be between two hundred and three hundred years old. Winds have buffeted this sentinel tree for so long that

OPPOSITE: *The Lone Cypress, an ancient sentinel standing guard over the rugged coastline, is a trademark of the Pebble Beach Company.*

now cement and guy wires are needed to keep it in place. Not far away is the Ghost Tree, now barely a stump bleached white by the sun and spray. These Monterey Cypress trees are part of native stands found naturally in two places only, Pebble Beach and Point Lobos. Trees are an important "crop" inside Pebble Beach, or "the forest" as locals call it. Each year, the Pebble Beach Company and its forestry department grows 200,000 seedlings in greenhouses to be planted throughout the five thousand acres.

During April and May, fences go up along Fanshell Beach and Cypress Point Lookout. Although the fences block a view or two of the coast, they are protecting a far more magical sight. Behind the temporary barriers, mother harbor seals teach their babies to swim and survive in the protected coves. The Pebble Beach Company cuts holes into the wooden barricades so visitors can watch the seals, but they admonish watchers to keep quiet and not disturb them. The wooden panels at the Cypress Point Lookout are painted with ocean scenes by local school children.

All of this shoreline and its marine inhabitants are now protected for the future by the creation of the nation's largest marine sanctuary. The Monterey Bay National Marine Sanctuary was established in 1992 after more than a decade of work by local scientists, politicians, and environmentalists. It is the fourth national marine sanctuary in California, and it covers nearly one-fourth of the Golden State's coast and more than forty-two hundred acres of the Pacific Ocean, its boundaries stretching from San Francisco to Cambria. For those who fought for the federal money to establish the sanctuary, there were impor-

tant treasures to keep safe. The Monterey Bay Canyon is ten thousand feet deep, which is deeper than the Grand Canyon: it's uncharted territory that scientists have called the "true last frontier." One marine biologist who has studied the Monterey Bay for more than twenty years says he feels "like an underwater astronaut" exploring things that have never been seen before. There are now about fifteen marine research institutions ringing the Monterey Bay, studying the diversity of species, both plant and animal, that float, cling, or swim in this protected bay.

This protected area of land and sea is much how Samuel Finley Brown Morse, the true founder of Pebble Beach, envisioned his creation. The grandnephew of Morse code inventor Samuel Finley Breese Morse, he was the manager of the Pacific Improvement Company properties in 1915. He wanted the forest left intact and dismissed plans that called for small lots developed on the shores of Pebble Beach. Instead, he turned to his friend Jack Neville to design a golf course that would overlook Carmel Bay. The result was the famous Pebble Beach Golf Links, which have won praise from golfers for decades, even while they grumble about their scores. Morse then decided to rebuild a log lodge that had burned down during the construction of the golf course. He designed an impressive new lodge that today is a cornerstone of the Pebble Beach Resorts. Morse eventually bought the Monterey Peninsula holdings of the Pacific Improvement Company, continuing with his plan to develop Pebble Beach with lots of greenery and open space.

Great forests of kelp grow along the Monterey Coast, offering hiding places and food sources for sea otters and other sea life.

Pebble Beach, for all of its estates, mansions, and resorts, is not just home to the wealthy. "A lot of people have lived here for a long time," says Lorraine Brownlee, who has lived in the "forest" for almost thirty years. "People we've met were stationed at Fort Ord during World War II and bought a lot or a house here." Brownlee says she and her husband actually bought in Pebble Beach because the property taxes were lower than nearby communities and the house was more spacious for roughly the same price. "We tell people we live in the poorer section of the forest," Brownlee says with a laugh.

Still, behind the gates, hidden in the hills, and shielded by the trees are some of the scions of business, the aristocrats of politics, and the household names of the big and small screens. Producer Merv Griffin, singer Paul Anka, actresses Kim Novak and Joan Fontaine, astronaut Alan Shepherd, and Eileen Feather of weight-reduction fame have all, at one time or another, lived in the area. Privacy is the watchword here. And sometimes it is only when one reads the obituary in the local newspaper that the final whereabouts of a celebrity becomes known.

The most famous celebrity of all in this area is, of course, Clint Eastwood, who speaks with pride about his home. "Something about it gets in your blood. You can travel around the world and when you come back, there's always a good home feeling here," says the actor. "I feel that way about it more than any other place I've been."

PACIFIC GROVE

The temperate serenity of the coastal town of Pacific Grove has been a drawing card for visitors since the 1800s. The restorative powers of this forest along the ocean attracted Methodists in 1875, who came here for their spiritual and physical health. The tranquillity and friendly atmosphere still entice people more than a century later; the current crop are Southern California transplants who want to give up the smog, congested freeways, and the alienation of a megalopolis for a seaside village that calls itself "the last hometown."

Mayor Sandy Koffman is one of those recent converts to Pacific Grove life. A visitor to the area for thirteen years, Koffman and her husband chose Pacific Grove when they set up their "electronic cottage," a home-based marketing firm. "It was the magic of the meeting of the ocean and the forest," says the effervescent mayor. As visitors, "we'd spend our last day with a picnic at Asilomar [State Beach] and watch the surf pounding on the rocks, listening to the gulls. When we decided to move, we wanted to be near that. And now we're a block and a half away." The small town has also attracted golfing great Johnny Miller and football legend Bill Walsh, who both recently purchased homes within the city's limits.

It's a city that inspires loyalty among its citizens. People try to shop in Pacific Grove–owned stores first, shunning the nationwide chain stores. And although it may be called the Monterey Bay Aquarium, Grovers are quick to point out that half of the aquarium sits inside the Pacific Grove city limits. You can experience the Monterey Bay first-hand, since Pacific Grove, unlike its neighbor Pebble Beach, doesn't charge to see the magnificent coastline, which harbors tidepools teeming with life.

PAGES 76–77: A gull soars over breaking waves along Pacific Grove's coast. You can rent kayaks and bicycles nearby for tours beyond the waves or along the oceanfront.
LEFT: *The Seven Gables Inn, one of a half dozen bed-and-breakfast inns in Pacific Grove, overlooks Lovers Point.*
RIGHT: *The sun sinks into the sea along Pacific Grove's Ocean View Boulevard. Only two houses are built on the ocean side of the roadway, so the rest of the coastline is clear for spectacular views.*

This diversity of aquatic life is studied at the Hopkins Marine Laboratory, a satellite Stanford campus in Pacific Grove since 1891.

Butterflies also find the Pacific Grove environs rejuvenating and life-giving. The mild winter season makes this coastal spot a yearly retreat for monarch butterflies, who travel up to a hundred miles a day from west of the Rockies and up into Canada to finally rest their weary wings in the branches of eucalyptus and pine trees here. But unlike elderly human "snowbirds" from such wintry states as Minnesota and Wisconsin who travel to Florida and Arizona every winter, the monarchs don't have a map. What makes their long-distance journey even more awe-inspiring is that these particular butterflies have never been to Pacific Grove, since several generations have lived and died since last year's butterflies began their arduous trek.

Pacific Grove calls itself "Butterfly Town, U.S.A.," and every October the school district glorifies the return of this precious flock with a parade. Children dress as Indians, jellyfish, and caterpillars, but only kindergartners get to wear the orange-and-black wings of the mighty monarch. The butterflies are so important to this community that the residents voted a tax increase in 1990 to buy land near the famous butterfly trees. A major tree replanting effort is underway so that these black-and-orange creatures have future branches to cling to, which protect them from the dense fog and sometimes gusty winds blowing in off the Pacific.

Winter visitors will have the best luck seeing these insects on warm, sunny days. Monarchs have trouble flying in temperatures below fifty-five degrees. On chilly days, look carefully overhead into the branches of the pines. What may look like a cluster of dead leaves might actually be thousands of butterflies tightly folded together, clumped en masse to conserve body heat. In the early spring, as the days become longer and the temperatures a little higher, the butterflies start doing what they came here to do: perpetuate their species. This is the time of year monarchs dance among the trees as courtships ensue. Because the butterflies are

oblivious to everything but the desire to reproduce, this is a very hazardous time for them. Pacific Grove residents have now put up "Butterfly Crossing" signs to help warn visitors to keep a careful eye on the ground for amorous monarchs. Finally, the butterflies leave Pacific Grove in mid-March, winging their way toward California's Central Valley and beyond, where they'll lay their eggs on milkweed plants. And the cycle begins again.

Throughout his life, Nobel Prize–winning author John Steinbeck returned to the quiet stillness of Pacific Grove. He was born in Salinas in 1902, and he frequently came to his family's summer home on Eleventh Street in Pacific Grove. After his first marriage, he moved to the family cottage, living on the stipend provided by his father. Here, Steinbeck worked on parts of *The Red Pony, Pastures of Heaven, Tortilla Flat,* and *In Dubious Battle.* As he became successful, he eventually moved from Pacific Grove, but he returned several times during his lifetime, sometimes to be refreshed, sometimes to hide. Perhaps Steinbeck's most fitting tribute to his love of Pacific Grove was his final one. When he died in New York in 1968, his ashes were flown back to Pacific Grove, resting two days in the cottage's garden before being buried in the family plot in Salinas.

Famed author Robert Louis Stevenson, during his journey to the Monterey Peninsula in the 1870s, was also entranced by Pacific Grove. He wrote that during a hike to the lighthouse, he'd never seen a place more dreamlike; he included his musings about this untouched beauty of the point of the peninsula in his short work *The Old Pacific Capitol.* Numerous modern-day authors, including mystery writers Dianne Day and Nancy Baker Jacobs, as well as Newberry Award–winning children's author Paul Fleischman, now pen their works while living in Pacific Grove. National Book Award–winner Eleanor Cameron, who lives in nearby Pebble Beach, uses Pacific Grove as the setting for her children's books.

OPPOSITE: *Monarchs travel hundreds of miles to roost in eucalyptus trees during Big Sur's winter.* RIGHT: *Pulitzer Prize–winning author John Steinbeck was born at this stately house in Salinas in 1902. The Steinbeck House is run by the non-profit Valley Guild.*

One of the first permanent structures in Pacific Grove was the Point Pinos Lighthouse. Built in the 1850s, its beacon first shone in 1855, warning seagoers of the rocky shores. It is the oldest lighthouse still in continuous operation on the West Coast, and today, visitors from all over the world come to visit. If you're lucky, you'll hear stories of the famous lighthouse keepers from Bruce Handy, a sea-loving volunteer who leads a small cadre of volunteers who keep the refurbished light-house and its windswept grounds gleaming. The lighthouse still boasts the original lenses and prisms, standing eighty-nine feet above sea level. Its beacon can be seen up to fifteen miles away.

The front parlor of the lighthouse is restored with needlepoint chairs and a fireplace remi-niscent of the era of lighthouse keeper Emily Fish, who operated the facility for more than twenty years beginning in 1893. Fish was called the "socialite keeper" because she enter-tained frequently, giving teas and parties. "Emily Fish had a chandelier that was candle-lit," says Handy. "The sparkles radiated over the room. It must have been magnificent, noth-ing like we have now." A sign near the parlor indicates Fish hired more than thirty men and discharged most of them as incompetent.

Several women have shaped Pacific Grove's history and architecture. At a time when a "woman's place" was in the home, Julia Morgan designed some of California's most impressive homes, among them William Randolph Hearst's estate at San Simeon. She also contributed her creative mind to the Asilomar Conference Grounds, blending the buildings effortlessly into the glistening sand dunes dotted with windswept cypress trees.

RIGHT: *The Point Pinos Lighthouse, built in 1855 and open for tours, is the oldest continuously operating lighthouse on the West Coast.*
PAGES 84–85: *Exploring tide pools is popular at the rocky coast near the Point Pinos Lighthouse in Pacific Grove.*

Lovers Point, today a popular spot for weddings and family outings, was once off-limits to the public, until mayor Julia Platt took an ax to its locked gate.

Julia B. Platt helped create the park at the other point of Pacific Grove's rocky shoreline. A noted scientist and a known eccentric, Platt moved to Pacific Grove in her middle age at the turn of the century. Alarmed that the beach at Lovers Point was shut off from the public by a padlocked gate, she marched down with her ax one day and chopped off the lock, opening the beach to all who wanted to frolic in the small cove. She then spent many hours planting, raking, and improving the park. She was Pacific Grove's first woman mayor and when she died in 1935, her body was set out to sea in a wicker basket, so she could join the ocean she loved.

However, it was Elmarie Hurlburt Dyke whom residents came to call "Mrs. Pacific Grove." Mrs. Dyke used the popular Lovers Point (which some say is called Lovers of Jesus Point) to revive a festival that locals are sure rivals a Fourth of July celebration. It's called the Feast of Lanterns and includes everything from a children's pet parade to street dancing in downtown to a seniors' tennis tournament. It occurs during the last week in July, and you can enjoy the Feast of Salads, the Feast of Chicken, and the festival pageant, in which thousands pack the beach carrying paper lanterns and candles. No one knows who first told the story of the star-crossed lovers who are portrayed in the play on the breakwater stage, but as in melodramas of old, the audience boos the villains and cheers the hero lustily. The final evening is capped with a spectacular fireworks show and the singing of "God Bless America," which was led by the formidable Elmarie until her death in 1981.

Mrs. Dyke first made waves in this coastal town when she fought to keep Pacific Grove as the only "dry" town in California. This was one of the few battles she was to lose, and in 1969, Pacific Grove allowed alcohol to be sold within the city limits, a far cry from the teetotalling days of the early Methodists.

In fact, Pacific Grove has a long religious tradition and twenty churches can be found within its two square miles. In 1875, a hundred acres of land were donated to the Methodist Episcopal Church to establish a Christian Seaside Resort. On August 8, 1875, the first camp meeting of about 450 people was held for three weeks in what is now downtown, sparking an annual event. For ten years Pacific Grove retained its character as a camp meeting ground with tents and cottages, mainly occupied in the summer. Now as you stroll along the streets of Pacific Grove that hug the bay, you'll see small cramped quarters where you can look over and see what your neighbor is cooking for dinner. But it was once more roomy, since only one tent was pitched in the sixty-by-thirty-foot lot and all cooking was done outside. In 1889, fourteen years after the campgrounds were established, thirteen hundred hearty souls decided to make Pacific Grove a permanent establishment rather than a tent city.

The town celebrates its Victorian roots each year with several events. During the second weekend in April, downtown is closed to vehicular traffic and the city hosts the Good Old Days, which includes a Victorian fashion show, an old-fashioned pie-eating contest, a quilt show with old and new handiwork, and lots of booths showcasing the latest arts and

crafts as well as the town's nonprofit organizations. The twentieth century is not left out of this celebration of days gone by. In recent years, Pacific Grove has hosted a police officer motorcycle competition with motorcycle cops from all over California roaring into town with spit-shined boots and gleaming chrome. One of Pacific Grove's three main thoroughfares is shut down so legions of officers on Harley-Davidsons and Kawasakis can perform their precision drills and burn rubber as judges look on.

Harbor seals lounge in the sun on rocks along the Pacific Grove coastline. Wooden sidewalks along Asilomar Beach allow visitors a chance to get a closer view.

Pacific Grove possesses a number of fine Victorian homes, many of which have been lovingly restored to their turn-of-the-century greatness. Owners have combed through junk yards, antique shops, and restoration magazines for years looking for that perfect treasure to complete their jewel piece of real estate. "We literally called all over the country looking for period pieces for our house," remembers Christie Martine, who remodeled her Fifteenth Street home. Most of the historic houses within the city are adorned with green-and-yellow plaques that display the year in which the house was built and the first owner's name.

Residents in this tight-knit community are fiercely protective of their town's character, and protecting sometimes turns into protesting. Almost every major building within the city's confines has controversy attached to it. When a developer proposed a shopping center with a McDonald's behind the high school, protests abounded, though the center was built in 1975. Some people have continued the protest silently for decades simply by never setting foot within the fast-food restaurant. Afterward, city leaders enacted a ban on any new fast-food outlets. However, downtown struggled to stay busy. "You could have shot a cannon down the main street," remembers downtown barber Gene Allen, about the sleepy shopping district. "They thought this town was going down the tubes and [development] would bring in 'undesirables.' But this town needed some waking up." When a downtown movie multiplex was proposed, it was only voted in by residents after there was a compromise agreement that only family films would be shown.

Most recently, city officials and citizens debated the merits of a proposed Taco Bell outlet in Pacific Grove. The proposal tried to get around the fast-food ban by claiming a taco was really a sandwich, which, not surprisingly, didn't fly in Pacific Grove. "That was a defining moment for our city," says Mayor Koffman. "We looked at designing the shop so it wouldn't look like a Taco Bell, but in the end we decided to rule it out." And since so much of Pacific Grove's future hinges on its Victorian past and small-town quaintness, "that decision is really going to shape our future."

At one time, Pacific Grove boasted of having one of the largest department stores in the West. One local paper bragged that nowhere else in the world was a store of its scope to be found in a community with as small a population as Pacific Grove. That was in 1935 and Holman's Department Store had already been a centerpiece of downtown since 1891. W. R. Holman's visionary goals for his town were realized in 1931, when two new floors, the fourth and fifth, were added. Mr. Holman constructed the floors to give local men employment during the Depression, and to show his confidence in Pacific Grove as a business location. Eventually, Holman's went out of business, only to be taken over by another locally run family business, Ford's Department Store. But the 1989 earthquake drove that chain to bankruptcy, and the storefront remained vacant for years until local owners rescued it at a Small Business Administration auction.

BELOW: *The twelfth
tee at Pacific Grove's
Municipal Golf Course,
one of the most affordable
courses in the golf mecca
that is the Monterey
Peninsula.*

OPPOSITE: *A walking
trail parallels Pacific
Grove's Ocean View
Boulevard. Tree aloe
and iceplant decorate
Hayes Perkins Park
along the waterfront.*

Today, the newly refurbished Holman's
sells fine antiques and collectibles. While
Holman's, with its pink walls and butterfly
stained-glass window, is the cornerstone of
Pacific Grove's downtown, you will get the
truest connection to that "last hometown" by
wandering through side streets, where converted cottages now house coffee bars, cafes,
thrift stores, and some of the more than forty
restaurants in town, which make up the
lifeblood of the local economy. A hearty
hello and an invitation to sit and visit are
not an uncommon greeting.

If you have a few minutes, stop by Gene's
Barbershop on Lighthouse Avenue. It's
adorned with tonsorial artifacts collected
over the years, and brothers Gene and Gordy
are always on hand, discussing the issues of
the day or giving their opinions about the
latest movies. You might also stop in at the
Red House Cafe and Miss Trawick's Garden
Shop, next to the post office on Lighthouse
Avenue, Monarch Knitting and Quilts on
Central Avenue, or Pepper's Mexicali Restaurant on Forest Avenue, other local favorites.

With luck and perseverance, Pacific Grove
won't grow much larger than it is now. The
people who have come here for the refresh-
ing sea air and the quiet stillness of the pine
forest don't want Butterfly Town to lose that
"last hometown" feel.

MONTEREY

Monterey is the cornerstone of the Monterey Bay area and the hub of the Central Coast; it's also known as the birthplace of the state of California. Once known as "The Sardine Capital of the World," Monterey has now been given the new title "The Language Capital of the World" because of the many educational institutions based here.

PAGES 92–93:

A waterside view of Fisherman's Wharf in Monterey, filled with shops and restaurants.
ABOVE: *An artist's dolphins leap and arch over Cannery Row, which John Steinbeck called "a stink, a poem, a grating noise."*
RIGHT: *Bands of clouds frame a quiet marina that still boasts a sizable commercial fishing fleet.*

But whatever it is called, Monterey's history is extensive, its beauty incomparable, and its economic base chameleonlike, adapting to meet the needs of a changing populace. It remains a city walking a tightrope, balancing preservation of eighteenth- and nineteenth-century landmarks with the inevitable changes of twentieth-century additions.

The first European to discover Monterey's beauty was Sebastian Viscaino. In 1602, he found this great harbor and named it for the Count De Monte Rey, who had sponsored the journey. Viscaino sent back such glowing descriptions of this sprawling, half-moon bay that the next explorers a hundred years later didn't recognize the magnificent haven and sailed right on by. Nearly 167 years later, Gaspar de Portola reached Monterey by a difficult, overland expedition. But the rough seas did not match the depictions of the secure

harbor noted in Viscaino's diaries. So Portola marched on to discover San Francisco Bay. Realizing that he'd gone too far, Portola and his expedition retraced their steps but still missed Monterey Bay, camping on Carmel Bay.

Disheartened, Portola returned to San Diego. But he was to try again. Portola and Father Junipero Serra, who was in charge of the Franciscan missions, finally rediscovered the beautiful sanctuary. The pair established the Presideo de Monterey Bay in 1770, six years before the fledgling country called the United States of America was formed.

The bay and its ocean canyon, which is as deep as the Grand Canyon, have always been the catalyst of life for Monterey. For two centuries, generations have fished the waters off the coast. And now, the bay and its beauty lures tourists from all over the world.

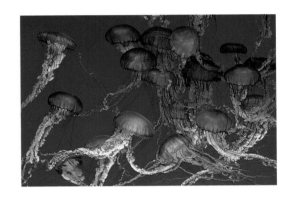

OPPOSITE: *Giant kelp in a three-story tank gives the impression of being in a sea forest.*

ABOVE: *Sea nettles (jellyfish) drifting lazily in the Outer Bay Gallery, which opened in 1996 at the Monterey Bay Aquarium.*

RIGHT: *These sea otters at the Monterey Bay Aquarium have the thickest fur of any mammal in the world.*

"We no longer catch fish, we catch people," jokes Monterey mayor Dan Albert. One of the biggest lures is the acclaimed Monterey Bay Aquarium. It opened in 1984 and pulled in more than two million visitors during its first year. Today, more than twenty million people have come through the door to gaze at the 300,000 creatures that live at the aquarium.

"I think the entire Aquarium exceeded our expectations in every account," says Executive Director Julie Packard. "It started from much more of an educational genesis. We were motivated to expand people's minds to think about the ocean, 70 percent of our planet."

The aquarium on Cannery Row re-creates the underwater life of the Monterey Bay: the kelp forest, the wetlands, the rocky tidepools, and the open sea. The three-story kelp forest "was our signature when we opened, and it really was an experiment," says Packard, a Central Coast resident since the seventies. The exhibit is nearly twenty-eight feet tall and was the first re-creation of a living kelp forest. Nearly fifteen hundred gallons of seawater are pumped into the tank, which undulates with kelp as sharks, sardines, and fish circle round. Scuba divers explain life inside this underwater forest as they hand-feed fish in daily demonstrations. The playful sea otters are another top attraction at the aquarium. A 55,000-gallon tank, two stories high, showcases these mammals, once considered almost extinct. Feeding times are very popular, and these furry beasts eat a lot. In the wild, a sea otter consumes 25 percent of its weight each day.

In 1996, a new wing of the aquarium opened to rave reviews. The tank in the Outer Bay wing boasts the largest window in the world at fifty-four feet long, and it holds one million gallons of seawater. This huge exhibit simulates the open ocean of the Monterey Bay from five to sixty miles offshore. This underwater slice of life includes soupfin sharks, barracuda, yellow-fin tuna, and ocean sunfish. Also a permanent part of this new wing is the largest collection of jellyfish in the nation. "The natural world is always changing," remarks Packard. "The world is not static and so our exhibits should not stay static."

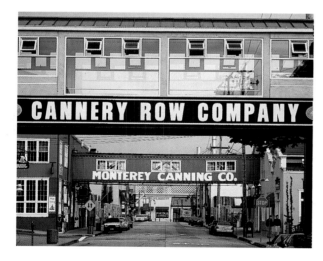

The aquarium was built on the site of the Hovden Cannery, the last operating sardine cannery on the row made famous by John Steinbeck. During the row's heyday, eighteen sardine canneries operated here. In the forties, it was said that if all of the sardines were laid end to end they would have reached to the moon and back. Not for nothing was Monterey once dubbed "The Sardine Capital of the World."

"Each boat could hold one ton of sardines. And there were three hundred boats out there," says historian Pat Hathaway. "Now, I bet you can figure out what happened to the sardines. . . . I've heard from old timers that the boats were so overloaded that they actually sank."

Dan Albert, who's serving his sixth term as mayor of Monterey, vividly remembers going to the canneries when he was nine years old. "There's a vision in my mind of going with my dad to pick up my mom who was working late, packing. There was an electricity in the air, with workers coming out and the steam in the air. That's what Steinbeck wrote about. But it did smell."

The Cannery Row that John Steinbeck wrote about is long gone. Today, you'll see T-shirt shops, fudge factories, antique stores, and even a Bubba Gump's Shrimp Factory, a theme-restaurant based on the film *Forrest Gump.* Many lament that the Cannery Row of today would have Steinbeck rolling in his grave. But Steinbeck friend and peninsula artist Bruce Ariss, who died a few years ago, scoffed at that notion. "Steinbeck would have loved what the row has become," he said in a 1989 interview. "He knew things change."

To learn more about life on the row before tourism took root, stop by the foot of Irving Street, where you'll find three original cottages that were rented by cannery workers. Each structure has been refurbished to represent a different era of the canning industry. Steinbeck fans will also want to visit the dark wood building right next to the aquarium at 800 Cannery Row, though you can't go inside. It once belonged to Steinbeck's friend Ed Ricketts, who collected marine specimens for the Pacific Biological Laboratory. The character "Doc" in Steinbeck's *Cannery Row* and *Sweet Thursday* was patterned after Ricketts. Ricketts was killed in a train wreck in 1948 at a railroad crossing at the end of Cannery Row, near the spot where the Monterey Plaza Hotel now stands. A bust of the marine biologist was placed at the site in 1997 on what would have been "Doc's" hundredth birthday.

Monterey has always taken special pride in celebrating its illustrious history. Five national flags have flown over the city. The Spanish flag waved until 1822, when Mexico gained its independence and raised its flag over the city. The Bear Flag of California was hoisted in 1846. And when California was admitted into the Union in 1850, the stars and stripes was flown. Though it did so only briefly, Argentina was the fifth country to raise its flag over Monterey. In 1818, a pirate named Hippolyte de Bouchard stormed into Monterey Bay and docked. The privateer and his band of three hundred men overwhelmed the local calvary of twenty-four men. For two weeks the buccaneers plundered the Presidio of Monterey, looting and burning. It took six months for the newborn city to recover, but it eventually did, becoming a thriving hub of commerce and the first home of California's constitution.

OPPOSITE TOP: *The Christmas season provides the contrast of California pastels, a palm tree, and a decorated pine on Monterey's Cannery Row.*

OPPOSITE BOTTOM: *The classic view of John Steinbeck's Cannery Row, where cannery workers once packed millions of cans with sardines.*

LEFT: *Morning over Moss Landing, where commercial fishing boats go out to collect salmon or squid.*

99

LEFT: *This mountain-top is nicknamed Fremont Peak for John C. Fremont, who raised the American flag here in 1846. The Monterey Peninsula sleeps under a shroud of fog in the distance.*
RIGHT: *Sunset colors illumine an elegant black oak standing tall in the Gabilan Range in San Benito County.*

There are a lot of firsts in Monterey's architectural history: the first brick house, the first theater, the first federal court, the first wooden frame building, and more. And the historic buildings have been well preserved. "The people who started the movement to save the adobes were brilliant," lauds Mayor Albert. "It's a great walking tour to all of those historical places."

That walking tour, the Path of History, takes you past forty buildings that shaped Monterey's development as a true core of commerce in the nineteenth century. You can purchase a map that briefly outlines this history and follow the sepia-colored tiles embedded in the sidewalks, which point out each historic structure. The Custom House near Fisherman's Wharf is California's oldest surviving public building. It was built in the 1820s when the Mexican government opened Monterey's harbor to foreign trade. Custom duties were collected here. On July 7, 1846, the American flag was raised here when Commodore John Drake Sloat captured Monterey and claimed California for the United States.

Just a few steps away from the Custom House is the Old Whaling Station Adobe, a private residence in the 1840s. Check out the whalebone sidewalk in front. This building once housed Portuguese whalers; today its lush gardens are a popular site for weddings.

California's first theater is on the corner of Pacific Avenue and Scott Street. Built first as a saloon and apartment house in the 1840s by

Jack Swan, it was converted to a theater at the close of the Mexican War. Ninety years later, the Troupers of the Gold Coast revived the old melodramas, which you can still see today as your sidle up to the bar at Jack Swan's Tavern.

The Larkin House on Calle Principal was once the home to Thomas Oliver Larkin, the first and only United States Consul for the Port of Monterey in California. He started construction of this architecturally interesting building in 1834. It's a unique combination of adobe, California redwood, and Cape Cod attributes. The house is filled with antiques from all over the world, which were collected by Larkin's granddaughter; she lived in the house until 1957.

Perhaps the greatest monument to Monterey's unique place in California history is Colton Hall, just a block up from the Larkin House. It was here that forty-eight delegates met for six weeks to decide the details of statehood. The convention wrote the new state's constitution, which was signed on the second floor on October 13, 1849. This resulted in California becoming the thirty-first state to enter the Union.

More than two million people come to Monterey every year to absorb history and soak up the winning combination of beaches and forests. But tourists often overlook an attraction that is well traveled by locals: more than eighty miles of hiking paths inside Veteran's Memorial Park in Skyline Forest. The Huckleberry Hill Nature Preserve was established when the army wanted to expand its Defense Language Institute, which abuts this forested area. Now, hikers can meander

through the trees, searching out some of the most spectacular views of the entire Monterey Bay. There's also a campground within Veteran's Memorial Park, a true bargain for an overnight place to stay.

The city of Monterey is careful not to overlook its residents' needs while luring tourists, so a recreation bike trail was developed for its citizens. The eighteen-mile trail spans some of the most scenic coastal areas in California, stretching from Asilomar State Beach in Pacific Grove to Castroville, the artichoke center of the world. Along the way, you'll pass some key landmarks: the aquarium, Fisherman's Wharf, a large grassy area with volleyball courts known as Monterey's Window on the Bay, and Del Monte Beach. The path, which is also open to walkers, follows in the train tracks along the old Southern Pacific Railroad right-of-way.

The barons who helped build the railroads in California had a special hand in developing the Monterey Peninsula as a tourist attraction. Charles Crocker, one of the Big Four railroad magnates, visited the peninsula in 1879 and was charmed. He dreamed of making Monterey a seaside resort and purchased seven thousand acres from David Jacks, who at one time owned sixty thousand acres of peninsula land. The centerpiece of Crocker's resort was the Hotel Del Monte and money was no object. Crocker spent $1 million, constructing the elegant edifice in just one hundred days. It opened its doors in June of 1880 and soon became a playground for the rich.

Visitors were treated to all the modern conveniences. There was hot and cold running water and telephones in every room. But just seven years after opening, a huge fire roared

OPPOSITE: *A Monterey cypress points the way to the historic Custom House Adobe, where the American flag was raised officially for the first time in California, on July 7, 1846.*
ABOVE: *The Pacific House, a historic adobe, is part of Monterey's Custom House Plaza.*

through the building, burning it to the ground. A second Hotel Del Monte opened for business in less than a year, and owners took advantage of the disaster to build an even bigger hotel, this one with enough room for seven hundred guests. Travelers continued to pour into the hotel from faraway San Francisco, brought for weekend getaways by Del Monte Express rail cars. The Del Monte offered guests a fifteen-acre lake, a private bathing pavilion on the beach, and even a golf course, the Del Monte Golf Course, which today is the oldest golf course in the West.

Today, the U.S. Navy is the only guest at the old hotel. During World War II, the hotel was leased to the navy as a preflight training center. It closed as a hostelry in 1951. The Naval Postgraduate School now occupies the converted buildings, educating officers of this country and our allies. A beautiful Arizona cactus garden was recently restored to its former beauty on the grounds, and it's well worth a visit.

The children of the Monterey Peninsula will tell you about their first choice for an afternoon of fun—Dennis the Menace Park, located near El Estero Lake. This former garbage dump has been transformed into a playground with some of the most imagina-

tive equipment. Youngsters spend hours crawling over the huge, black locomotive, jumping up and down on a suspension bridge built over soft sand, or wiggling down the wavy slide. The park was the brainchild of the Jaycees, a national civic organization, in the 1950s. They contacted Monterey resident and world-famous cartoonist Hank Ketchum and enlisted his help. When the park opened in 1956, after four years of fundraising, begging, bartering with, and wheedling the community, several hundred children marched from Colton Hall to the new playground. Today, hundreds of kids swarm over the playgrounds each day, screaming with delight. Nearby, you can also rent paddleboats to explore El Estero Lake. Recently, the city of Monterey stocked this man-made lake, and anglers of all ages flock to its shores for an easy catch.

Though anglers may have an easy time in Monterey, the commercial fishing industry there is just a shadow of its former glory. Today, the fleet trolls for squid rather than sardines. In a good year, fishing families can make a living harvesting salmon from the sea, but it is a struggle. Fisherman's Wharf is still a great

place to buy fresh fish, but now businesses on this famous pier are trying to land tourist dollars rather than fish in their seine nets.

The downsizing of the fishing industry and the loss of Fort Ord's huge military influence is forcing Monterey to reconfigure its economic base. California State University at Monterey Bay is California's newest university, opened in 1995 on former Fort Ord land, which was ordered closed by the military's base closure committee in 1990. City leaders are working to enhance the educational endeavors on the Monterey Bay, which supports eighteen institutions, including the Army's Defense Language Institute, the Naval Postgraduate School, the Monterey Institute for International Studies, and the Moss Landing Marine Lab. While city leaders appreciate the economic support these facilities bring, Mayor Albert says, "It's the cultural diversity we'd really miss, an even bigger asset."

Monterey's goal is to continue to balance on that tightrope, preserving its beauty and heritage while continuing to thrive as the axis of the peninsula first praised three centuries ago.

Monterey marina as
viewed from Wharf #2.
The average time spent
on the waiting list for
a berth is upwards of
seven years.

SEASIDE

The largest city on the Monterey Peninsula is Seaside, with a population of nearly forty thousand. Finally incorporated in 1954, it had been on the drawing board just sixty years before. In 1887, Dr. John L. D. Roberts envisioned Seaside as a complement to Crocker's Hotel Del Monte resort. Roberts wanted his resort available to the working man, so he bought 150 acres of the Rancho Noche Buena and subdivided it into parcels. In 1890, he established the Seaside post office, where he was postmaster for the next forty-two years. But Roberts's vision was not shared by others, and as late as 1920 the town of Seaside still had just one paved road and a handful of houses.

Today, Seaside is an ethnically rich city still struggling from the closure of Fort Ord. "We still have a ways to go yet in our economic recovery," says Jacqueline Lambert of the Seaside/Sand City Chamber of Commerce.

The city has taken control of the two golf courses on Fort Ord, Blackhorse and Bayonet. "The thing that pleases me about the golf courses is that they're still affordable to people in our community who've been playing them for years," says Lambert. Seaside is trying to get its share of the tourist pie while still offering quality services to its residents. A large Embassy Suites hotel recently opened within city limits, and other hotels are planned. A man-made lake off Del Monte Avenue, used by toy motor boat captains and bird watchers, is named after Roberts. Nearby, visitors can also enjoy a beautiful Russian Orthodox church, Saint Seraphim's at Laguna Grande Park. The park offers boardwalks and playground equipment for children. Though the town suffers from some of the common difficulties of most urban locales, it is very much a pivotal part of the Monterey Bay region.

A blazing sun settles down for the night, as seen from Marina State Beach.

SANTA CRUZ

Some things happen only in Santa Cruz. A man dressed as a clown—Mister Twister—was arrested for putting money in expired parking meters. A planned Fourth of July visit by a huge navy ship sparked protests. A beauty pageant was disrupted when one finalist turned on the contest and condemned beauty pageants as demeaning to women.

PAGES 110–111:

Coastal contrasts are evident during minus tide at Davenport Beach. Santa Cruz County has twenty-nine miles of beaches to enjoy.
ABOVE: *Professional surfers compete in an annual surf competition off the Santa Cruz shore. The two most popular surfing spots are Steamers' Lane and Pleasure Point.*
RIGHT: *Bright blooms encircle the moored boats at the Small Craft Harbor in Santa Cruz.*

Santa Cruz County is known for having an eccentric citizenry. But while offbeat stories make headlines, it's the medley of differences that endears this county to its residents. Santa Cruz is special because of "its diversity—the natural beauty from ocean to mountains, the diversity of terrain, the redwoods and the sea," says Marty Bargetto, a third-generation wine grower. "There's a diversity of people here, too, cultural and artistic. The endeavors by people here are vast—music, dance, wine."

The pundits and those who don't really know will tell you that Santa Cruz County is a liberal county. And if you stopped only at the University of California at Santa Cruz (UCSC) or at the Pacific Garden Mall and never strolled beyond those boundaries, you might agree. But there are also conservatives, sometimes hidden in the hills, sometimes not so silent, who call Santa Cruz County home. As one old-timer put it, "There wouldn't be controversy if you didn't have two sides to a fight."

Much of the bickering and debate over the years has centered on the beachfront. The twenty-nine miles of shimmering beaches and the vibrant marine life off the coast have been Santa Cruz's calling card for generations. "It's about as close to America in the 1950s as you can get," says Sharon Finneran Rittenhouse, an Olympic silver medalist who settled in Santa Cruz. "There are no high rises. That's lucky and special for those of us who live here."

As the thermometer creeps above seventy degrees, the Santa Cruz waterfront comes to life. It's a place that sparkles. The waves break gently and run up the beaches, which are dotted with sunbathers, volleyball players, and seagulls looking for a free handout. Stately palm trees line Beach Street, where in the peak summer season you'll be hard pressed to find a parking space and gridlock

is not uncommon. Inline skaters glide by as you stroll along the greenbelts, and you are sure to be treated to impromptu serenades from ever-present bongo drums.

Amid these sun-washed activities, the Southern Pacific freight trains still grind their way down the railroad tracks, their rending screeches mingling with the screams from the Giant Dipper roller coaster at the Santa Cruz Beach Boardwalk.

The boardwalk is California's oldest amusement park. In 1904, promoter Fred Swanton opened a casino and boardwalk that mirrored the Coney Island and Atlantic City parks of his youth. It was the same year that Venice Beach in Southern California opened, and some people were worried about the competition. The Northern California park only operated twenty-two months before a fire swept through the beachfront attraction, burning it to the ground in 1906. Swanton saw this as an opportunity to build something even bigger and better. The boardwalk reopened in 1907 on a mile-long stretch of beach and has been a family favorite ever since.

The Giant Dipper roller coaster is the star of the show. More than 45 million people have hopped aboard this wooden coaster since it first opened in 1924. Enthusiasts gasp as the coaster ascends seventy feet in the air, providing a great view of Monterey Bay. Then you hear the shrieks as the cars hurtle over the wooden supports at speeds up to fifty-five miles an hour. But the Dipper is not the oldest ride. That honor goes to the carousel, which was brought with its hand-sculpted

OPPOSITE: Flags flutter over feathery waves in front of the Old Casino portion of the Santa Cruz Beach and Boardwalk, which was built in 1907. RIGHT: Intricately carved seahorse sentries stand guard at the Santa Cruz Boardwalk, where more than forty rides enhance family fun.

BELOW: A march of arches frames an empty portion of the Santa Cruz Boardwalk. Neptune's Kingdom was originally The Plunge, but was rebuilt after the 1989 earthquake. It's now an amusement center with miniature golf and games.

horses to the boardwalk by the famous European woodcarver Charles I. D. Loof in 1911. Both rides have been designated National Historic Landmarks by the U.S. National Park Service.

The boardwalk celebrated its ninetieth anniversary in 1997 and is still packing them in. Kids flock to shoot the Logger's Flume or to smash into one another in the bumper cars. And one tradition hasn't changed no matter what generation you belong to—the boardwalk and beach offer a perfect chance to see and be seen.

In the fifties and sixties it was called cruising. "From the time I got my license in 1960, cruising was the thing to do," says Pete Bachtel, a native of Santa Cruz. "In the summer, it took half an hour to get from one end of Beach Street to the other because of the bumper-to-bumper traffic. You got to see girls who came over from Fresno, Modesto, and Bakersfield. Santa Cruz kids got to make friends with all of them."

Santa Cruz still depends on those valley residents, who escape the hundred-degree swelters in the San Joaquin Valley by vacationing in the playgrounds of Santa Cruz County. The number-one industry here is tourism, with agriculture and high tech a distant second and third. Santa Cruz County boasts three-hundred sunshine-filled days a year, while averaging thirty-one inches of rain. Such people-pleasing weather offers a great recipe for outdoor fun.

Locals often gloat that they are always within walking distance of a state park or beach. There are more state parks in Santa Cruz than any other county in the state. And the

OPPOSITE AND RIGHT: *Crowds have been finding summer fun at the boardwalk in Santa Cruz since Fred Swanton opened this seaside amusement park more than ninety years ago. It is the oldest operating amusement park in California and is a state historical landmark.*

granddaddy of this illustrious family is Big Basin Redwood State Park. Dedicated in 1902 as the first state park in California, its eighteen thousand acres were set aside to preserve the redwoods from logging.

Of the one hundred miles of Big Basin trails, perhaps the most famous is the "Skyline to the Sea" trek, which is an unbroken path from the mountains to the sea. This park off Highway 9 near Boulder Creek provides something for everyone, with both treacherously steep trails and easy footpaths for families. There is overnight camping if you want to sleep among

the *Sequoia sempervirens* coast redwoods. Reservations are strongly recommended.

Many see those evergreen spires of Henry Cowell Redwood State Park as cozy. Historians say a hollow trunk once served as a campsite for General John C. Fremont while he was a lieutenant. This controversial figure in American history once lived inside this tree and even built fires there. Fremont was a leader in the Bear Flag Revolt in 1846, when a small band of men proclaimed an independent republic of California.

After just one month, they learned that Mexico and the United States were at war, so Fremont and his men joined up with Commodore John Sloat to fight for true independence. He was later named the military governor of the state, but he disobeyed orders and was court-martialed, though he was eventually pardoned by President Polk. Today, the Fremont Tree is one of the most visited destinations in this popular park. The smallest child and the oldest grandma will be able to maneuver an easily accessible circular path. Pick up

Family fun is on tap at the Natural Bridges State Beach in Santa Cruz, with a wide sandy beach and nearby picnic grounds. This area is also a site for monarch butterflies to rest during the winter. OPPOSITE: *Picturesque Sempervirens Falls on the Sequoia Trail in Big Basin Redwood State Park, one of many sites worth visiting in this park, established to protect the trees from overzealous logging.*

TOP: *Witness more than two thousand years of magnificence: the "Father of the Forest" tree along the Redwood Trail in Santa Cruz's Big Basin Redwoods State Park.*
BOTTOM: *Moss covers the remains of once towering redwoods in Big Basin Redwood State Park, the first state park in California.*
RIGHT: *Experience serenity along a walking trail in Henry Cowell Redwoods State Park.*

a printed guide and match up the numbered attractions to learn more about these skyscrapers of the plant kingdom.

One of the newest parks on the Santa Cruz menu is Wilder Ranch State Park, first opened to the public in 1989. The park showcases well-preserved remnants of history within its five-thousand acres. On your way to Wilder Ranch along Highway 1 north of Santa Cruz, you'll pass rolling hills that slide into the sea. On these bluffs overlooking the majestic Pacific, lush green grass is nourished by fog pockets, which cling to the hillsides like ship barnacles. Throughout the last three centuries, dairy farmers have taken advantage of nature's bounty, running herds of cows in

these heavenly pastures. Visitors to the Wilder Ranch today can see family homes from the Spanish mission period to the 1890s, when the ranch was a highly innovative dairy. There's also a working blacksmith shop, a massive barn (which accommodated all those bovines), and an impressive fern grotto carved into beachfront cliffs. Docents dressed in period costumes are on hand to give tours of the ranch and demonstrate some of the old-time skills. Children are especially delighted by the preservation of the ranch complex, in particular the farm animals, who don't do any more than "moo" or "neigh" when guests get a little too close. Historic games such as rolling hoops, stilts, and bubbles are also on tap for the youngest visitor.

LEFT: *A solitary fisherman at Four Mile Beach in Santa Cruz County.* ABOVE: *The main ranch house in the historic district within Wilder Ranch State Park is one of many distinctive buildings on this still-active farm.* OPPOSITE: *One of Santa Cruz's many parks, the Wilder Ranch recalls an agricultural past with this barn and buggy.*

*A yellow-tinged big leaf
maple overhangs Aptos
Creek in the Forest of
Nisene Marks State
Park. This area was
almost clear-cut a
century ago, but today
you can see regrowth.*
OPPOSITE: *Aptos Creek
tumbles through the
Forest of Nisene Marks
State Park, not far
from the epicenter of
the 7.1 Loma Prieta
earthquake of 1989.*

And if you haven't seen enough of the majestic redwoods, don't miss the ten thousand acres of the Forest of Nisene Marks, established in 1963. If you bike or jog within the heavily forested area, you'll find it hard to imagine that a century ago this land was practically clear-cut by logging operations. But new second- and third-growth redwoods have germinated and flourished through the years, providing a shady getaway from the stresses of modern life.

On October 17, 1989, ancient forces far deeper than the roots of these sequoias changed the face of Santa Cruz County. In this park, not far from the Aptos Creek Trail, was the epicenter of the 7.1 Loma Prieta earthquake, the result of the slow drifting of the earth's tectonic plates. At 5:04 P.M. on a warm Tuesday afternoon, the San Andreas Fault experienced a fifteen-second temblor that toppled two-story brick buildings like children's blocks. Six people died and scores were injured in Santa Cruz County. The Pacific Garden Mall became a triage center. Downtown looked like a war zone.

In the aftermath of the quake, more than two dozen downtown buildings had to be demolished, with construction crews bringing down what little the force of nature had left standing. Perhaps the most poignant demolition came on October 26 when a wrecking ball shattered the walls of the Cooper House, built in 1894 and a survivor of the 1906 quake. The lot where it once stood remains empty. "The Cooper House was the one building that everyone wanted to save," says Neal Coonerty,

The Santa Cruz Post Office and nearby town clock, the site of numerous community gatherings, watches over one entrance to the Pacific Garden Mall.
OPPOSITE: *Flowering cherry trees grace the Pacific Garden Mall in Santa Cruz.*

a downtown merchant. But Coonerty, who was mayor in 1993 and served on the city council, says the earthquake did more than shake the ground. He says it also shook up the way people viewed the business community. "People really saw that we could become a bedroom community for the Silicon Valley. They wanted to rebuild. They began to appreciate the business community and not think of them as the 'establishment' or the enemy."

The rebuilding process began just three weeks after the October quake. A committee decided to put up huge white tents to act as "temporary" stores for the important Christmas shopping

season. Coonerty's Bookshop Santa Cruz survived in that tent for three years. "The third year was very difficult. There was construction going on so it was dusty and the parking was gone," Coonerty remembers. "People were remarkably loyal despite the fact that the retail space was inadequate." Though the scar of the earthquake can still be seen, the Pacific Garden Mall is reborn, alive with restaurants, antique and artist's boutiques, kitchen stores, an organic grocery store, and of course, the ubiquitous coffee-houses. Professional offices on second and third floors overlook a steady stream of humanity enjoying the rebuilt mall.

And when the sun sets, the sidewalks don't automatically roll up. Santa Cruz nightlife is centered on Pacific Avenue, and the Catalyst is the place where it all began in the sixties. A one-time hangout for hippies, you'll now find yuppies cheek-to-cheek with grannies as they pack in to listen to great music. The Kuumbwa Jazz Center has been centerstage for jazz lovers for twenty years, booking some of the top names in the industry. A newcomer to the music scene, Palookaville is a smoke-free nightclub and juice bar. And if singing the blues is your calling, stop by Moe's Alley Blues Club on Commercial Way.

LEFT: *A brilliant coastal vista of the sandstone headlands south of Davenport in Santa Cruz County provides an excellent place for whale watching from November to March.* RIGHT: *Windsurfers ride powerful waves on the gusty Santa Cruz County coast, here at Davenport Landing.* BELOW: *The power of the sea in action never stops along the coastline south of Davenport, an artist enclave off Highway 1 in Santa Cruz County.*

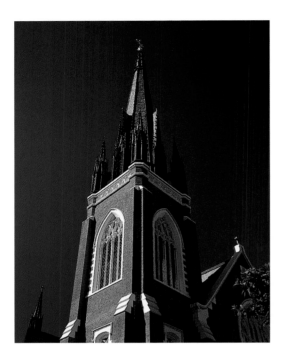

Saint Patrick's Catholic
Church in Watsonville
was heavily damaged
by the 1989 Loma
Prieta earthquake, but
has since been rebuilt
after a long, expensive
restoration project.

WATSONVILLE

The other large city in the county, Watsonville is still recuperating from the October 1989 temblor. Its downtown area, built around a plaza with a quaint gazebo, has suffered since the earthquake shook the Ford's Department store into rubble. That flagship store, started in Watsonville in 1852, was rebuilt, but the local chain of eight stores, which suffered $18 million in damages from the quake, couldn't recover and closed, leaving a hole in a once vibrant downtown.

"I remember when the downtown was alive and well," says Milt Amaral, who grew up in Watsonville and now lives in Sacramento. He recalls "the big day when Kim Novak and Jimmy Stewart stayed in the Hotel Resetar while filming *Vertigo*." And he says the Miramar Grill was a magnet for "people who came from Santa Cruz and the Monterey Peninsula. The waiters had white shirts, black pants, and bowties. The service was impeccable and the food was great. Those were the good old days."

"Watsonville is at a crossroads, struggling with an identity crisis," admits Police Chief Terry Medina. Watsonville, with a population of about thirty thousand, has always been in the shadow of its northern neighbor, Santa Cruz. "There's a yin-yang sense between the two communities," muses Neal Coonerty.

Just two years after John Watson founded the town in 1852, Watsonville petitioned the legislature to be removed from Santa Cruz County. More than 140 years later there's still discontent over political policies. "Santa Cruz has a no-growth policy. It doesn't want Watsonville to expand," says Medina, who has lived in Watsonville since 1982.

While Santa Cruz reaps tourist dollars, Watsonville harvests crops for its economic base. The Pajaro River, before it flows into the Monterey Bay, leaves an alluvial plain of rich soil ideal for growing strawberries, apples, and cut flowers. You may have sipped a Watsonville product this morning with breakfast. Martinelli's Cider and Soda Works was established in 1868 and has been making juice and sparkling cider ever since. Rose enthusiasts may also be familiar with another Watson-ville locale, Roses of Yesterday and Today. This specialty nursery sells rare and unusual roses all over the world through its catalog.

And now leaders in Watsonville are trying to lure tourists to the Pajaro Valley to see agriculture in action. A country crossroads map will guide you to "U-pick" farms, where a family can load up on strawberries, raspberries, pumpkins, and apples. A wonderful place to spend an hour or two is the Gizdich Ranch, where you can devour strawberry shortcake or the tallest apple pie you've ever seen. Just a short drive away, Corralitos Market & Sausage Company tempts you to stop. They smoke more than a dozen types of sausages, including Cheesy Bavarian, Chicken Santa Fe, and the more traditional hot links and linguiça.

OPPOSITE RIGHT:
Apple trees bloom near
Corralitos in southern
Santa Cruz County.
Nearby Watsonville is

home to Martinelli's
Cider and Soda
Works company.
BELOW: *Hundreds of*
acres of strawberries are

planted near Watsonville
in Santa Cruz County.
Other crops grown in this
area include cut flowers
and nursery stock.

Watsonville, the second largest city in Santa Cruz County, is a prime agricultural center. Strawberries are the county's number-one crop.

This covered bridge once protected travelers near Felton, one of several communities in the Santa Cruz Mountains. OPPOSITE: *Palms frame the tower of the Mission Santa Cruz, established in 1791.*

AROUND SANTA CRUZ COUNTY

Watsonville's small-scale businesses aren't the only agricultural endeavors with growing national reputations. Vintners in the Santa Cruz Mountains are quickly gaining in stature. The mountains support about a hundred acres of wine grapes and more than a dozen wineries, many open for tastings. "There's no [wine-growing] place where mountains and sea come so close together," says Marty Bargetto, marketing director for his family's winery in Soquel. "What that yields is grapes of distinct complexities."

The wineries are all small and clustered in the mountain communities of Boulder Creek, Felton, and Bonny Doon. Fine pinot noirs, chardonnays, and zinfandels are produced in this region. "Not a grape grown here goes outside the county," says Bargetto. If you maneuver your way through the mountains during the Christmas holidays, most of the wineries will be dressed in finery as old-fashioned as a Currier and Ives print.

Santa Cruz is the second smallest of California's counties, and it is one of the state's original twenty-seven counties. It was called Branciforte when the Golden State came into the Union in 1850. But the area was

first settled by friars who came to convert the Native Americans. The Santa Cruz Mission was organized in 1791. In the beginning of the nineteenth century, the verdant, tree-laden mountains were the sustenance of the community. Logging in the San Lorenzo Valley was rampant. Millions of redwoods were harvested, leaving the hillsides bare.

The ocean's bounty was also being collected. By the beginning of the twentieth century, waves of immigrants were arriving in Santa Cruz to mine the sea just as they had done in the old country. "The Italian fishing industry started here in Santa Cruz before it started in Monterey," says Sis Olivieri, whose parents came to Santa Cruz in 1913. "It was a relaxed life, no stress like there is now." Sis, an octogenarian who looks decades younger, still lives in her family home overlooking the wharf with her younger sister, Rina. "I was named after my father's [fishing] boat," says Rina Carniglia.

The two sisters are proud of the changes that have come to Santa Cruz during the seven decades they've lived there. During Prohibition, the siblings remember hiding barrels of booze in the garage. "Our folks knew all of the cops, who used to warn us about the raids," says Sis, laughing. "We didn't have a lot of money," says Rina. Her sister, Sis, picks up the story without missing a beat. "We used to make our own scooters out of old skates and we'd skate all over these hills," she says, pointing to the hills that overlook the boardwalk.

But the sisters say that when summer ended so did the excitement. "Labor Day came and Santa Cruz died," says Rina. "I think the university was a wonderful thing," says Sis. "Santa Cruz needed something [to make] this a year-round town."

The University of California opened its Santa Cruz campus in 1965 and it did change the complexion of the county. Most thought the changes were good, but some were not as enthusiastic. "It brought a lot of the cultural positives that major cities have," says Coonerty, whose sister was in the first class at the university. But others feel that UCSC merely swelled the area with a transient, disruptive population, since students come and go each year. UCSC is home to some of the finest programs in the arts and sciences, including the Long Marine Lab, which uses the nearby sea as its source. There's an eighty-five-foot

ABOVE: *Elephant seals haul themselves out of the sea during the winter at Año Nuevo State Reserve on the San Mateo County coast.*
LEFT: *A full-grown bull elephant seal at one* *of the largest breeding grounds in California, Año Nuevo State Reserve.*
RIGHT: *Greyhound Rock Beach in Santa Cruz County offers anglers a place to cast their lines.*

BELOW: *On the University of California at Santa Cruz campus, established in 1965, several buildings are remnants of the historic Cowell Ranch, where Henry Cowell ran cattle, logging operations, and lime kilns.* RIGHT: *The Mark Abbot Memorial Lighthouse and*

Santa Cruz Surfing Museum, dedicated by Abbot's parents after Mark was killed in a surfing accident, displays one hundred years of local surfing history. OPPOSITE: *Surfing Steamers' Lane, one of the premier places in Santa Cruz to shoot the curl.*

whale skeleton there, as well as sea lions and dolphins. UCSC is known for being an experimental university, so it's not surprising that some of the nation's leading research on organic farming takes place on its twenty-five acre farm and four-acre garden. The university also has a year-round flower show in its arboretum, showcasing plants from around the world. The university hosts a Shakespeare Santa Cruz festival, which is known for modernizing some of the Bard's most famous plays.

The Pacific is still the wonder that draws people to Santa Cruz. Steamers' Lane is a legendary place to catch a wave. You can even visit the first museum dedicated to surfing at Lighthouse Field, overlooking Steamers' Lane. Learn how Hawaii's surfing royalty introduced their pastime to locals decades ago, and explore one hundred years of surfing history, with vintage boards, including the "shark attack" surfboard. The museum, which opened in 1986, was sponsored by nationally known photographers Chuck and Esther Abbot as a tribute to their son, Mark, who was killed in a surfing accident. California's twelfth lighthouse, completed in 1869, once sat on this point of land. The original building was a two-story frame house with a Fresnel lens mounted in a wooden cupola on the roof. The grounds of Lighthouse Field also are an overwintering site for monarch butterflies.

Other popular coastal enclaves within the county include Aptos, which Native Americans called Awatos, or "where the waters meet." The name honors the spot where two creeks join before traveling together to the bay. The village of Aptos is small, stuffed with cute little stores and quaint restaurants. The Old Bayview Hotel dates back to Aptos' early days as a logging town. It's an Italianate palace that now is a bed-and-breakfast inn.

On the first floor, the Veranda restaurant serves an excellent brunch. Beachgoers will enjoy the string of beaches that start at Aptos and ring the bay south toward Moss Landing. Seacliff State Beach has a small nature center and a short pier that ends at the *Palo Alto,* a concrete-hulled boat that briefly sailed in 1919 before breaking up in winter storms. The shipwreck then dropped anchor to became a dance hall and cafe. For a stroll down a long beach, check out Manresa State Beach and even farther south, the Sunset State Beach, which has ninety campsites.

*The colors of the
rainbow are painted
on the Capitola Venetian
Hotel, perched on the
Capitola City Beach
in Santa Cruz County.*

Capitola was founded more than 125 years
ago by a German immigrant, Frederick
Augustus Hihn, who called the beachside
community Camp Capitola. Hihn was a
businessman who is said to have named
his town as a ploy to get the state capitol
moved to his part of the coast. Hihn brought
progress to much of the Santa Cruz area,
building a wharf in Capitola and bringing
the Santa Cruz–Watsonville Railroad into
the area. The esplanade hugs the beach with
colorful stores, delicious seafood restaurants,
and art galleries. Capitola celebrates its seaside resort status with its annual Begonia
Festival. Think of it as the Rose Parade on
water. Townspeople fill Soquel Creek with
flower-draped floats, wiring fifteen thousand
blooms to the pontoons in a matter of hours.
This September event also boasts a sand castle
contest. There's an art and wine festival, as
well, where thousands cram the esplanade to
drink in sun, the fruit of the vine, and works
created by local artisans.

Santa Cruz residents are proud of their home, which Neal Coonerty says offers "the diversity of Christian churches and Deadheads" in one town. And, says Sharon Finneran Rittenhouse, "Whenever you feel blue, you can get in your car or walk to see the ocean. It's one of the most beautiful places in the world. I hope I never leave."

Houses and shops are in close proximity in Capitola, a seaside town of eleven thousand people.